STUDY FOR SURVIVAL AND SUCCESS

Guidenotes for College Students

SANDER MEREDEEN

P·C·P
Paul Chapman
Publishing Ltd

Illustrations and cover illustration ©
Patrick Welch.

Cover design by ACE.

First published 1988 by Paul Chapman Publishing Ltd.
144 Liverpool Road
London N1 1LA

Typeset by Burns & Smith, Derby.

Printed in Great Britain by
Athenaeum Press Ltd, Newcastle upon Tyne

British Cataloguing in Publication Data
Study for survival and success: guidenotes for college students.
1. Study techniques, Manuals – for higher education institution students
I. Meredeen, S. (Sander), 1928–
378′ .17′ 02812

ISBN 1 85396 047 0

F G   4

For Emily and Joanna Brogan
and for my godson
Daniel Welch
with every good wish for
survival and success
as you – and your
contemporaries –
set out on
your college
journeys

Lies

Telling lies to the young is wrong.
Proving to them that lies are true is wrong.
Telling them that God's in his heaven
and all's well with the world is wrong.
The young know what you mean. The young are people.
Tell them the difficulties can't be counted,
and let them see not only what will be
but see with clarity these present times.
Say obstacles exist they must encounter,
sorrow happens, hardship happens.
The hell with it. Who never knew
the price of happiness will not be happy.
Forgive no error you recognise,
it will repeat itself, increase
and afterwards our pupils
will not forgive in us what we forgave.

Yevgeny Yevtushenko

from *Selected Poems of Yevgeny Yevtusheuko*, translated by
Robin Milner–Gulland and Peter Levi (Penguin Modern European
Poets, 1962), © Robin Milner–Gulland and Peter Levi, 1962.
Reproduced by permission of Penguin Books Ltd.

Contents

FOREWORD

The cost of student failure (exam resits: repeat years: drop-out) has always been high but is now becoming intolerable – first, to the students themselves; second, to their parents, families and dependents; third, to institutions of higher education; and fourth, to society which can simply no longer afford such unnecessary waste of human potential.

This book aims to reduce those costs by helping you – the student – to cope better with your entire college experience. It derives from the author's own experience of educational failure and success.

As an 11+ failure, I long felt conspicuously inadequate. As a mature student of 25 at the London School of Economics, I was a fearful freshman. Graduating with 1st class honours in economics and political science, I shared with others the excitement of discovering hidden talents somewhat late in life, and devoted the next twenty years to the development of human resources in manufacturing industry.

As an even more mature student, back at the LSE, tackling a masters degree at forty-eight, I underwent an acute crisis of identity: what am I doing here, reading in the library, when I ought to be working? Shortly after, I was recruited by my own head of department to become a teacher – first at the LSE, latterly at the University of Strathclyde. For twelve years I have taught, advised, researched, counselled, written, published, broadcast and consulted widely in the private and public sectors, finding still wider sources of personal growth, development and fulfilment.

As an active member of the burgeoning international movement of teachers, trainers, advisors, counsellors and administrators, devoted to enhancing the First Year Experience, I offer these *Guidenotes for College Students* everywhere – regardless of age, sex, race, colour, religion, nationality, economic status or other distinction. May you find help here to survive your college studies and go on to success and fulfilment, in whatever terms you choose to define them.

Finally, I express my warmest thanks and appreciation to Alex Main (University of Western Australia, Perth) for transporting me to Columbia SC in January 1985; to John N Gardner, Jerry Jewler, Stuart Hunter and Richard Lawhon (Freshman Year Experience Centre, University of South Carolina, Columbia SC) for their generous hospitality, and friendship; to my six contributors for their sangfroid in writing under severe time constraints, and to Patrick Welch for his wonderfully witty illustrations.

Sander Meredeen
Glasgow, July 1988

Notes on the Contributors

*With some revelations on their own efforts to study,
survive and succeed at college*

Sander Meredeen failed his 11 + examination; suffered a wartime education; completed two-and-a-half years' National Service in the Royal Navy; spent four vegetable years at the Ministry of Education; attended WEA evening classes in Economics; entered the LSE as a mature student of 25; graduated with 1st Class Honours; spent 20 years as an Industrial Relations Manager with British Steel and Ford Motor Company; returned to the LSE as an even more mature student of 48; completed his MSc in Industrial Relations and Personnel Management in 1975; joined the LSE teaching staff in 1976; published his first book on Industrial Relations in 1980; and became Senior Lecturer and Deputy Head, Department of Industrial Relations, University of Strathclyde Business School in 1984.

Yvonne de Barr's interest in psychology began as she observed her three sons grow and develop. Her studies in human growth and development were further stimulated by her involvement in the Pre-School Playgroup movement. This was followed by an Open University degree, majoring in Psychology. After several years teaching mature students in a college of higher education, she completed a counsellor training course. She now lives and works in Essex counselling and teaching counselling-related subjects.

Shirley Meredeen began her career as a junior on *The News Chronicle* followed by twenty years of journalism in London and beyond on a variety of daily, weekly and monthly newspapers and magazines. Her second career in student welfare began intuitively in 1970 at Brentwood (Essex) College of Education, then at the Polytechnic of North London where she was Accommodation Officer. She joined City and East London College in 1978 where she is Senior Student Services Officer. Having learned her job by bitter experience, her own academic development came later, following the graduation of her two sons. She claims some fame in being one of the slowest students to complete her Open University degree, having studied for her BA in two halves, from 1971–74 and from 1981–84. She added theory to experience by completing her Diploma in Counselling Skills at South West London College in 1986.

Roslyn Taylor took an Honours Degree in Psychology at Glasgow University. After a brief sojourn as a social worker in Greenock, she completed her M Phil and worked for ten years as a Clinical Psychologist in the NHS where she also researched the use of psychology in Health Centres. For three years she was a TV presenter with Scottish Television which included a series on fitness and health. In 1982 she set up the Taylor Clarke Partnership (formerly Leimon Taylor Consultants), specialists in motivation, communication and stress management. She recently pioneered Weight Management, a programme for effective weight loss and helped found Lifestyler, a company specialising in health and fitness courses. She consults widely at home and abroad on health, fitness and stress management and is currently writing on those themes for *The Scotsman*.

Craig McDevitt read Modern History at St Andrews University; took his Certificate in Education at Dundee College of Education; became a student counsellor in London; completed his Certificate in Student Counselling by part-time study in 1982; and was appointed Student Counsellor at the University of Edinburgh in 1983.

Alwyn James was born and bred in Wales; read History at Cambridge; married an Irishwoman; edited business journals for 10 years in London; travelled widely in Eastern Europe; went to Scotland in 1970 and became involved in all things Scottish; edited the magazine 'Scotland'; published three books — *Scottish Roots* (1981); *Other Men's Heroes* (1982); *Raring to Retire* (1982); was appointed Press Officer to The Royal Bank of Scotland in 1983 and designated Chief Press Officer in 1987.

Ian Easton was born in Scotland where he has lived and worked all his life. He graduated MA from Glasgow University; spent 11 years in education; completed an extended lecture tour of the United States; was appointed UK Head of Communications for an American multinational; became responsible for all management training in a major steel company; taught for 20 years at the University of Strathclyde Business School; and now practises as an independent consultant in human resource management.

Patrick Welch was born in Essex where he attended the local Comprehensive School. He completed a Foundation Course at North Essex School of Art before going on to the Norwich School of Art where he took 1st Class Honours in Illustration and Graphic Design in 1987. He now lives and works in Chelmsford (Essex) as a free-lance professional illustrator.

Preface

This book is about making the most of some important years of your life. Whether you see education as an obstacle race or, as I would hope, a not-too-steep staircase, you can use help from those who have been that way before. The author of this book is such a person. His widely-ranging career in industry and university has given him a lively and sympathetic insight into other people's problems. Unlike most authors, he is on the side of the reader, probably because he has stayed a student himself. Read what he has to say, enjoy him – his wit and his wisdom. I know him well and know that you will like and value his gentle advice.

Graham Hills
DSc, LLB, FRSE
Principal and Vice-Chancellor
University of Strathclyde
Glasgow, Scotland
June 1988

Introduction: so, you're about to start college?

These guidenotes are for students who are about to start college, or who are already there: bright students and average students; black students and white students; men students and women students; traditional students and mature students; home students and overseas students; students of every subject, in every faculty – these guidenotes are for you. We hope you find them relevant and useful, no matter what course of study you intend to pursue – at college, university or polytechnic. For simplicity, we shall refer simply to 'college' study throughout these guidenotes.

If you're about to start – or have just arrived at college – you'll probably be feeling both excited and anxious: excited at the prospect of embarking on a great adventure of living and learning with other students, of being free to make your own decisions and to lead your own life; but anxious, too, about how well you'll cope with all the demands that are about to be made on you:

- Mental demands (Am I really bright enough for college?)
- Physical demands (Do I have the energy to see the course through?)
- Psychological demands (Have I got what it takes to be a student?)
- Social demands (How will I survive on my own away from home?)

These guidenotes set out to deal realistically with those anxieties. They explain what a student's life is really like: what's expected of you; how to cope better with your studies; how you can get more out of life as a student; how to do really well. In short, how to survive and succeed as a college student. These guidenotes can't anticipate every single problem you may ever have to face as a student. But they've been compiled by a team of college teachers, consultants and counsellors with many years' experience of helping students cope with the problems and difficulties most students encounter during their time at college. They tell you most of what you need to know for student survival and success. Let's start with *the bad news* first.

IT'S GOING TO BE HARD WORK

If you're not prepared to work at college, you're going to feel miserable and you're almost certainly going to fail. Even if you scrape through your exams, you'll probably feel that you wasted much of your time. Going to college is an adventure – one of the most exciting opportunities you'll ever have in life. To make the most of those opportunities you'll have to work . . . but not all the time. To work well at your college studies, you must be reasonably healthy. That means becoming and staying fit for the mental, the physical, the psychological and the social demands that will be made on you – or rather, the demands you'll make on yourself. So, be ready for hard work! Second:

YOU'RE GOING TO FACE LOTS OF DECISIONS

Most students particularly look forward to being independent, finding things out for themselves, making their own decisions. That's fine, as long as you realise you may not always be fully equipped to make some of the most difficult decisions in your life so far. For example, how should you allocate your time at college? How many hours a day should you spend in the library? When should you stop work and have fun? Where can you meet like-minded people and make friends? What should you do if you get stuck with a work problem? How do you cope when you run short of money? Or when you're ill? Or when you become emotionally distressed over some personal problem – such as a friendship that goes wrong? These guidenotes offer suggestions on all these and related questions. Third:

YOU WON'T BE HAPPY ALL THE TIME

College represents a transition to a more independent world where things don't always work out as we intend or hope. There will be disappointments and setbacks as well as progress and achievement; frustrations and annoyances as well as satisfaction and enjoyment. But you can learn to handle and to cope with these adult emotions. In part, that's what college is for. You might describe college as a 'half-sheltered learning environment': more demanding than school, less demanding than the 'real world' of competition for jobs and careers, promotion and success. So . . . what's the *good news*? First:

MOST STUDENTS REALLY ENJOY COLLEGE

Provided they make a successful transition from home, school, employment or unemployment to college life, most students find they derive a great deal of satisfaction from their studies. New concepts and theories can be intellectually stimulating and emotionally exciting. Even hard work can be enjoyable when you're working alongside other students who are struggling with first essays, or note-taking or exam revision – just like you. Because college life is essentially sociable, you learn to share your problems – intellectual puzzles, philosophical doubts, emotional confusions and perplexities – as well as your convictions and certainties. College is a place where you learn to analyse ideas, handle concepts, evaluate theories and arguments – but, above all to share those ideas, concepts, theories and arguments with others. Second:

YOU'LL MAKE LOTS OF NEW FRIENDS

During your college life of shared experience, you'll meet fellow students, teachers and other college staff, some of whom may become lifelong friends. Former students often keep in touch for the rest of their lives. But making friends is never as easy as it sounds. How do you make friends in a lecture hall with perhaps over a hundred other students? The answer is that lectures are not for making friends. There are other places and other times for that purpose: coffee-breaks; lunchtimes; college sports; music and drama; discos; and social, cultural and political clubs and societies. Most colleges have a thriving social life. Make sure you don't miss out! It's vitally important not to feel lonely or become isolated at college. Third:

YOU'LL GROW IN SELF-CONFIDENCE

The best part of college life is intensely personal: the sense that you're being intellectually stretched; that you're growing as a person, developing skills and abilities you never knew you possessed. That personal growth helps to build your self-confidence. It should sustain you for the rest of your life.

But you'll also learn humility: the ability to stand back and admire the skills and gifts of others – students and teachers, more able than yourself, who will demonstrate a capacity to handle complex ideas and concepts better than you'll ever manage to do. That's part of college life as well – the self-respect that comes from knowing you've explored the limits of your own capabilities, and can live more cheerfully within your own limitations.

Of course, you'll make your best effort. But study skills do not come naturally to most students. Like all other skills, they have to be learned. How do you get the best out of an hour's lecture? How do you sustain concentration in the library for hours at a stretch? How do you prepare to write your first essay? Trickier still, how do you handle your teachers' critical comments on your written work? And how do you score higher marks next time? In each chapter of the following guidenotes, we deal with all these points and many more. Fourth:

YOU'LL NEVER REGRET IT

Whatever the outcome of your college studies – whether you graduate with a brilliant degree or simply achieve an honourable pass in your exams – you'll never regret your time at college. In simple, practical terms, the most interesting jobs and the best salaries go to people with good college qualifications. Of course, there are exceptions: self-made men and women who somehow get to the top by the force of their own personality. But for most of us, a college education is the passport to a worthwhile and rewarding career. There's also that special sense of well-being that comes from setting yourself a difficult but attainable target – like completing a course of college study – and achieving it by your own efforts. So . . . what do these guidenotes cover?

Chapter 1 deals with the college experience Settling into college takes time. You probably won't really feel comfortable until you've worked through those early feelings of being 'a stranger in a strange land' – away from your familiar landmarks and routines of home, school or former workplace. This chapter explains what college is for. It goes on to examine the nature of human learning. It tells you how to find your way around college – as the first step towards survival and success.

Chapter 2 deals with accommodation You'll never survive and succeed at college unless you have somewhere reasonably comfortable and affordable to stay. Where do you find such accommodation? How should you use it? How much should you pay for it? That's what Chapter 2 is about.

Chapter 3 explores the world of students, teachers and other college staff Students comprise all kinds of conditions of men and women. How well do you relate to other students? Can you learn to get on with them? And what about teachers? Are they really human? What sort of life does an academic lead? Is it possible to make friends with college teachers? And those other, somewhat mysterious, members of college staff? What do they all do? You need to discover the specialist services other college staff have to offer students.

Chapter 4 deals with a top priority task: choosing subjects and class options Of course, you may already known exactly which subjects you intend to study and which classes you'll take. But you may be surprised and even disconcerted by the range of options facing you. You need to choose wisely – and not leave those choices too long. Chapter 4 deals with the art of making sensible choices.

Chapter 5 is about managing your time at college When you begin college, time seems to stretch ahead endlessly. But you soon find yourself up against deadlines – for deciding subject options; for submitting written assignments; for entering examinations; and so on. Then there are so many lectures, meetings, tutorial papers, essays, sports events, discos and parties – quite apart from eating and sleeping – to be fitted into a college week, which still has only 168 hours. College time is your most valuable resource, so you must learn how to manage it. Chapter 5 suggests ways of improving your time management at college.

Chapter 6 offers advice on developing good study habits Once you've settled in, found your way around, met some fellow students and attended your first classes, you must get down to your studies. There's nothing magical or mysterious about good study habits, but you need to understand how best to study in order to survive and succeed with your college learning. Chapter 6 is all about the why, where, when and how of successful study.

Chapter 7 is about getting the best out of lectures This is one of several chapters dealing with regular features of college life. A college lecture may seem just like school – or it may seem a very foreign and strange experience. Are lectures a waste of time? How can you sustain concentration when lectures are so boring? You listen but what can you learn from lectures? Chapter 7 tries to answer those questions.

Chapter 8 deals with more effective reading Every student – no matter what their subject – must master the art of reading faster and more effectively. There are so many books and so little time. How do you go about improving your reading skills? How do you train your memory to retain more of what you've read? We have some practical suggestions to offer here.

Chapter 9 suggests better ways of taking notes from reading As you read, you'll want to take notes. What's the secret of good note-taking? What do you do with notes once you've taken them?

Chapter 10 is about getting the most out of tutorials/seminars Having attended your first lectures, done some reading and taken some notes, you'll be invited to your first tutorial or seminar. What's the difference? And how should you prepare yourself for small – group learning sessions? What if you've been asked to open the discussion? How do you set about it? Chapter 10 makes a number of practical suggestions.

Chapter 11 is about better college writing In due course, you'll sit down to write your first college essay or writing assignment. You'll never forget that essay – or the mark you achieved! What is your teacher looking for in a first essay? What's meant by effective college writing? How do you learn to do better next time? It offers many helpful hints to college writers.

Chapter 12 is devoted to critical thinking and problem solving. To write well, you need to think straight. You may think you already know how to think. But can we improve our thinking skills? What's meant by critical and creative thinking? How can these skills be applied to your college studies?

Chapter 13 tells you how to pass those exams – and stay human Before you know it, the first year is nearly over and you're facing your first exams. You give up late-night parties. You start to worry whether you've done enough work to survive. Your heart beats faster. You may not get to sleep at night for all those facts churning about in your brain. Chapter 13 tells you how to prepare for exams; how to improve your exam technique; what examiners are looking for in a good exam answer; and how to raise your exam performance.

Chapter 14 offer guidenotes on writing a research dissertation or project report It's addressed to students whose course includes some element of research or a project on which they're expected to submit a report. That may seem a daunting prospect. It's quite different from writing an essay or a tutorial paper, or even an exam answer. You're more likely to be working alone and will need to be much more self-reliant. Chapter 14 suggests ways in which you can plan and carry out your research and present an acceptable report, on time.

But enough of this academic talk! Surely there must be time to relax and enjoy yourself at college? There certainly is. But to enjoy yourself, you need to be fit and stay healthy. (Some college activities can be very un-healthy . . . We leave you to decide which.)

Chapter 15 questions whether you are fit for studying? Does going to college mean giving up alcohol? Will you inevitably become an alcoholic? Certainly not! Physical and mental well-being depend to a remarkable degree, however, on sound nutrition – which means enjoyable eating and drinking, at moderate cost, with the occasional blow-out! Chapter 15 offers nutritious food for thought.

Chapter 16 deals with tobacco and other addictive substances It will probably make you reach for your 'fags' – that is, if you're still a smoker. Why shouldn't students smoke if they feel like it? What could be nicer on a summer's evening, than sharing a bottle of wine and a reefer? Surely all this propaganda against soft drugs is exaggerated? Anyway, if you can't experiment at college, when can you? Chapter 16 addresses these questions in an adult and positive way.

Chapter 17 is on sex, love and dreams This chapter seems destined to become the best-thumbed section of this book. We have no reason for saying that – other than the experience of our own lives. The guidenotes we offer will certainly be anxiously scanned for advice on some of the most pressing problems of college life. We deal with the ecstasy and the agony of personal relationships. We deal with venereal disease, with urino-genital infection and AIDS. Not to do so would be irresponsible. But we also try to deal sympathetically with non-medical but no less-painful problems – feeling jealousy or experiencing recurrent disturbing dreams. Is it all really worthwhile? We know you'll read Chapter 17 to find out.

Chapter 18 rounds off this area with managing stress Most college students look after themselves fairly well and stay healthy. But one feature of college life that seems to afflict nearly all students is stress – not least at exam times. In Chapter 18 we examine the whole question of mental fitness. We explain what stress really means, how to recognize your own stress symptoms and how to deal with them. We recommend all students – without exception – to give Chapter 18 close attention.

Chapter 19 insists that money matters College doesn't come cheap. Even if your tuition fees are paid by some grant-awarding authority (and by no means all students have their college fees paid), you will still have substantial outgoings on fares, lodgings and meals, quite apart from books and clothes and entertainment, however modest. Chapter 19 faces up coolly to the whole question of money: who has it and how to get some, how to organize a student budget, what to do when all's spent. Read it now . . . before you get too deeply into debt.

Chapter 20 turns to students facing special problems We've chosen to deal with seven particular groups: (1) the majority; (2) mature students; (3) students with disabilities; (4) overseas students; (5) black students; (6) women students; and (7) gay and lesbian students. Mature students may seem better adjusted and happier at college than most traditional students, but they face special problems and may need extra help. Overseas students may have special problems – with language perhaps, or food or climate or social customs. Disabled students have obvious problems – like access – to deal with. But less-obvious problems can also affect their study. The same is true of black students, women students and gay and lesbian students. Chapter 20 discusses some of those problems and suggests ways of dealing with them.

Chapter 21 tells you where to go for advice and help Sooner or later, every college student needs help and advice with some personal problem. Not necessarily an intimate problem, but personal to them. You may have run out of money or have nowhere to stay. You may be feeling lonely or ill. You may not be coping with your study or with other people in your life. You may be in trouble with the law. You may feel you can't face it all – and be ready to give it all up. *Don't wait* until these problems become too difficult to manage – read Chapter 21 now. Sooner or later, you're going to need the advice we offer!

Chapter 22 is all about career choice and job search Whether you're one of those charmed creatures who seem to go through college without encountering a serious problem – or one of those who seem always to be in the wars – you'll need to start thinking soon about your future career. Where do you go for sympathetic careers' guidance? Do you really know what sort of career you're likely to be good at? Do you know how to prepare a good CV (curriculum vitae or résumé) of your life? You'll certainly need to brush up your interview skills.

Chapter 23 rounds off these guidenotes with some practical suggestions on staying on at college Suppose you've caught the learning bug and feel like staying on? What can you study when you've finished your present course? What's the value of a post-graduate qualification, and when is it best done? Are there research opportunities for well-qualified students? Will further study or research enhance your future job prospects?

We conclude by asking: So, what did you get out of college? We very much hope and believe you'll get a great deal out of college, besides your paper qualification. But in case you're still wondering whether to accept that college place or start at university or polytechnic, we take you through some of the benefits you might reasonably expect to get out of college life:

- A lifetime's love of learning?
- A passport to a well-paid job?

- An intellectual training?
- A set of social skills and graces?
- A sentimental education?
- Some really worthwhile friendships?

We trust these guidenotes will be of practical help in securing these benefits. As you set out on this voyage of self-discovery – the adventure of college life – you should be under no illusions: it won't be all plain sailing. There are hazards for the unwary, inevitable squalls and calms ahead. We're sure you'll find the voyage worth while – wherever it takes you! These guidenotes will have served their purpose if they keep you off the most dangerous rocks. We suggest you keep them handy throughout the voyage.

1 The college experience

Saturday 23 April. *Between five and six we set out. We had a very good journey, and we chatted a good deal. I got to Oxford about six. The ideas which I had conceived of that noble university were realised when I saw it . . . I sauntered about for an hour before I could find Sir James Macdonald . . . He had with him [four students who] talked of learning too much; and in short were just young old men without vivacity. I grew very melancholy and wearied. At night I had a bed at the Blue Boar Inn. I was unhappy to a very great degree.*
James Boswell's *London Journal* (1762–3)

This chapter tries to do three things:

1. To investigate what's meant by 'the college experience'.
2. To examine the nature of human learning.
3. To suggest ways of finding your way around college.

WHAT'S COLLEGE FOR?

It may be a new experience for you – but students have been going to college for at least two-and-a-half thousand years! So we should probably begin by asking what college is for and reviewing the various arguments that surround it.

From Plato's Academy, in fifth-century BC Athens, to the latest government report on higher education, experts have been pronouncing on the value of college education – what it contributes to the development of individual character and what to society. Despite these centuries of thought, there's still no clear consensus on what the purpose of college is – or should be. Two schools of thought predominate. Adherents of the first school advocate 'pure education' or 'education for its own sake'. They argue that college provides an intellectual and moral training that equips a person for the ups and downs of life – personal, social and professional. On intellectual development, they cite the example of the British Civil Service that, since the Northcote–Trevelyan Reforms of 1854, has filled its policy-making posts with graduates, selected for their demonstrated capacity for independent thought, their ability to learn and to perform to high intellectual standards, without regard to academic specialization. The permanent secretaries in charge of many government departments are arts graduates who have risen through the ranks of the meritocracy to become Knights of the Realm and heads of Oxbridge colleges, simply by virtue of their intellectual training, character, hard work and a modicum of good luck. They mastered their profession, as it were, along the way.

Since adherents of this first school regard college as primarily an intellectual training ground, they stress the inherent educational value of such subjects as classical languages (Greek and Latin), political philosophy or English literature, all of which encourage the development of sensitivity, subtle and flexible reasoning, intellectual ingenuity and the willingness to see all sides of an argument.

Adherents of the second school bewail Britain's poor economic performance and diminished standing in the world, which they attribute in large measure to the lack of relevance in much that is taught in colleges. They claim to have discovered a close relationship between the rate of growth in Gross National Product and the type of college education favoured by Britain's economic competitors, arguing that the nations that prosper most are those that prepare their students best for the 'enterprise culture' of the late twentieth century.

Adherents of this second school favour the teaching of such vocational subjects as economics, accounting and law, science and engineering, computing and information technology – because these subjects are all directly relevant to the world of work. They would not proscribe the teaching of fine art, archaeology or music – but would much prefer to see British colleges turning out many more vocationally-trained graduates in science, technology and business management. If, then, we define the first aim of college as being *to provide an intellectual training in the useful arts*, we might leave both schools to continue their debate on what exactly constitutes usefulness in a rapidly-changing economic and social world.

The second aim of college has to do with *the encouragement of individual difference and the development of personality*. Here there is more general agreement. Education is seen as a process of nurturing individuality, of fostering distinctive qualities that already reside within each individual. College should therefore encourage students to become more autonomous, to develop greater self-awareness, to fulfil their potentiality by exerting effort and will-power to achieve their highest standards of attainment – whether it be the completion of a first-year essay, an honours dissertation or a doctorate of philosophy. This self-actualization ('becoming your best self') is widely seen as the most valuable benefit of college study. To put it another way, 'Education is what's left when you've forgotten all you ever learned'.

'The college experience' might, therefore, be described as a voyage of self-discovery, self-development and preparation for self-fulfilment. It's an experience that is undeniably concerned with the acquisition of facts, the deepening and broadening of knowledge and the development of character. It therefore has everything to do with the psychological growth, development and fulfilment of the whole person – with a unique biography, unique gifts, unique problems and a unique contribution to make to society. You don't study these subjects at college: they are the incidental, unintended, beneficial result of submitting yourself to 'the college experience'.

LEARNING CAN BE FUN

If all this sounds heavy and pompous, it's worth pointing out that college experience also offers intellectual excitement. In short, learning can be fun – provided you equip yourself sensibly for the voyage of self-discovery. You must be prepared to take some risks and be willing to learn from your mistakes. Paradoxically, you should see the voyage of self-discovery as *a shared experience*, in which you seek to increase your own competence and self-confidence by means of mutually-rewarding relationships with your fellow students, your teachers and other members of college staff.

As the Introduction said, studying for survival and success will be hard work but it should not be drudgery. There should be room for relaxation, for sport, for social and cultural activities as well as academic work. Colleges do not admit students unless they seem capable of sustaining and successfully completing their college courses – and of entering fully into college life. Despite careful selection, however, a proportion of students drop out of college each year for a variety of personal reasons: exam failure; illness; and family or other personal circumstances. Some drop out is probably inevitable. But it is also very costly – to the individual, to the college and to society generally.

Chapter 6 offers specific advice on some aspects of developing good study habits, but it's important at this early stage to understand something about human learning. What exactly do we mean by 'learning'? How does the brain work? Does everybody learn in the same way, or in different ways?

1. Learning is a natural – one might say an instinctive – human activity. All animals appear to have some capacity to learn from experience. But humans have a far higher capacity than lower-order animals.
2. Learning in humans begins at birth and continues until very old age or death, unless brain incapacity intervenes. So, learning is not quite the same as education.
3. Learning is a process whereby knowledge, skills and attitudes are acquired or modified in such a way that human behaviour is more or less permanently changed. We learn by acquiring new ideas, concepts and values – or by displacing old ones.
4. Un-learning is more difficult than learning – because we become habituated to thinking or feeling in certain ways over time. So, it takes longer to eradicate old learning (bad intellectual habits) than to acquire new learning (good intellectual habits).
5. Learning, like all other forms of human behaviour, is a motivated activity. We do not learn unless we wish to learn – although some individuals still find it difficult to learn, despite their strong motivation, because of some learning block. Such learners need special counselling.
6. Individuals learn in different ways. There is no such thing as 'best practice' when it comes to human learning. Whatever works best for the individual is the best way to learn.
7. There appear to be few limits to the human capacity to learn. The brain – like any other human organ – can tire. But there is no such thing as limited brain capacity. Most humans use only a small fraction of their total useful brainpower.

8. Learning is both a conscious and an unconscious human activity. We may pick up (i.e. learn) bad habits (e.g. nail-biting) without realizing it. We absorb (i.e. learn) a great deal of French vocabulary, grammar and syntax by listening to people speaking French without making a conscious effort to learn the language. Other subjects – like calculus or computing – cannot be learned without some conscious effort.

FINDING YOUR WAY AROUND COLLEGE

If you are to enjoy the college experience to the full, you need to lose no time in finding your way around college. The sooner you 'sus out' what happens at college, the sooner you'll settle down and begin to enjoy the college experience. Students who drop out or who fail their college courses are often those who failed to come to terms quickly with their new environment and to make the necessary personal adjustments to fit into that environment. You must adapt to suit the environment – the environment can't change just for you!

First, you should recognize that you need to be much more self-reliant than you've ever been before. Nobody will come looking for you if you don't get up in the morning or fail to appear for a 9 o'clock lecture. If you persistently fail to appear, your teachers will note your absence and the college authorities will probably institute enquiries. But, generally speaking, you're expected to be a self-starter at college.

Second, you need to master the geography of your college and learn how long it takes to get to and from various locations. There's nothing worse than arriving fifteen minutes late for a lecture or laboratory practical to find out that other students have stolen a march on you. That does not mean giving up lectures. It means organizing yourself to arrive at places on time, without external promptings. Perhaps you need to buy a reliable alarm clock, or give up early-morning TV and settle for hearing the day's news on radio. (See Chapter 5 for further detailed advice on managing your time at college.)

Third, we need to remind ourselves that the college experience comprises your own self-discovery in the company of other members of the college community. Every college is a community of scholars – teaching, learning, reading, writing, experimenting, offering advice and consulting one another – sharing the college life together. You must discover how and when to take part in that sharing. But you must also find ways of working alone and becoming more self-reliant. Suppose, for example, you've been given a problem to work on by one of your teachers. How long should you spend on that problem alone – and when do you turn to fellow students to share ideas on possible solutions? There are no hard-and-fast rules. You must simply strike a sensible balance between working alone at your problems and collaborating with others. But, however you begin, you should end up by sharing your own findings, your own views and conclusions with others.

To share with others, you need to know where to find them. Just as you may resent being disturbed in the college library, so fellow students don't enjoy being interrupted in the middle of some important piece of work. In any case, the library is not the place to talk through mutual problems: much better to meet in the refectory, cafeteria or dining-room. We suggest you find out where your newly-acquired friends and acquaintances tend to gather at different times of the day. In that way you won't feel cut off and isolated at college and will know where to seek out help when you think you need it.

You should develop your own reliable method of recording the names of people and places; college buildings and their quaint room-numbering systems; opening and closing hours of libraries, college and faculty offices; student-welfare and advisory-staff offices' telephone numbers. You don't need to become a slave to Filofax – but you probably do need a college diary or alphabetical address book with space for telephone numbers, etc.

Finally, you should set aside some time every week to take stock of your work and your progress. Try designating the same time every week – like Friday or Sunday evening. Keep a record of how you spend your time and what you've managed to get done during the previous week. Then develop a weekly list of the tasks you hope to achieve during the week ahead. Number the items and try placing an 'urgency rating' against each item: *** for those books already overdue at the library; ** for that essay to be presented by next Monday; ** for the tutorial paper you're committed to give next Tuesday; * for less urgent items, like the laundry or shopping you must try to have done by the weekend.

SUGGESTIONS FOR FURTHER READING

Open University, *The Idea of a University* Milton Keynes: OU Press: Arts Foundation Unit, 1970.

Newman, J.H., *The Idea of the University*, University of Notre Dame Press, 1982.

2 Accommodation*

> *My first encounter with Cambridge (in 1936) was with Mrs Stubbins, my landlady, whose house overlooked Midsummer Common. Her hair was done up in curl papers and wire clips and she wore a faded apron. Her manner was impersonal and she seemed to regard my arrival with some relief, as if a problem had been solved. She showed me to my rooms and called my attention to a postcard on the mantlepiece from my tutor . . . Mrs Stubbins' manner suggested that I was in for trouble.*
>
> H.S. Ferns, *Reading from Left to Right: One Man's Political History* (1983)

This chapter tries to do three things:

1. To stress the importance of a roof over your head.
2. To outline the range of possible student housing.
3. To explain the advantages and disadvantages of each.

*This chapter was kindly contributed by Shirley Meredeen, BA, MASC, Senior Student Services Officer, City and East London College, to whom any comments or queries may be addressed directly at Student Counselling Services, City and East London College, Pitfield Street, London N1 6BX (01–638–4171).

A ROOF OVER YOUR HEAD

Are you a stereotypical middle-class undergraduate, driven to the
university or polytechnic of your choice by your proud parent,
complete with hi-fi, food hamper, alarm clock, extra socks and pleas
to phone home regularly? If so, you'll have probably booked your
place in a hall of residence, your grant will arrive on the first day of
term, you'll be ready to enjoy Freshers' Fair and soon settle down to
studies in the library.

Perhaps you're less well-prepared, with fewer resources and had to
scrabble around to find your college place through Clearing? Or a
mature student, apprehensive about coping with study after such a
long absence, worried about managing financially and missing your
children and family?

Does your college have enough accommodation to offer?
Each new academic year, the media presents a pretty accurate picture
of the accommodation crisis, with students having to doss down in
seminar rooms while hundreds of unhoused students search for a more
suitable base.

The forced camaraderie and freedom from normal constraints may
have its attractions. But the lack of sleep, washing facilities, privacy
and the delay in settling usefully into your studies is not a good start to
college life. This period can be profoundly depressing and some
students withdraw at this point. It's impossible to start studying
seriously until you've found a roof over your head that suits your needs
and allows a clear head for studying.

The realities of student housing
All universities and polytechnics (and most other colleges) have an
accommodation office for student housing. Some offices send out
information automatically while others wait for you to approach
them. This office should always be your first point of contact. In fact,
it's probably wise to contact the accommodation office when
considering a particular college because their housing policy may
affect your final choice of where to study.

Accommodation offices provide information on the types of
housing available locally, on college policy regarding priority for halls
of residence, comparative costings, lists of housing in the private
sector and considerable back-up on your legal rights, housing law, etc.
The latter are particularly important because the 1989 Housing Act,
changes the status of landlords and tenants considerably, affecting
security and rents.

Where supplies are available and you're offered a choice, it's sensible to check out the accommodation on offer. You need to be realistic about the amount and type of belongings you'll bring with you. For example, you may have a choice of accommodation on campus or off, with meals or without. There are advantages and disadvantages of each and you may need to see them all before deciding.

THE RANGE OF STUDENT ACCOMMODATION

Halls of residence

Colleges with their own halls can normally house only a small proportion of students. Most give priority to first-year, some to final-year students, but few can house all students throughout their course. Some offer rooms at a meals-inclusive charge, others are increasingly self-catering with shared kitchens. Most have individual rooms with washing facilities; others have rooms for sharing. Many of the newer halls have some rooms suitable for the disabled, who normally get priority to stay throughout the course.

With some halls on campus and others off, you need to consider the pluses and minuses: the first eliminates travel time and expense but you may feel isolated from the wider community; the second involves travel time and fares but provides more choice of shops and entertainment, with an escape from the enclosed campus.

Halls normally charge a term's rent in advance. That's an immense chunk of grant to allocate early on but it allows you to budget carefully the meagre remains. A distinct advantage is that the costs are clear and explicit, inclusive of heating and hot water, without extras – except perhaps for laundry.

Until the property-price boom, halls were often more expensive than private housing. But, unless colleges change their pricing policies radically, halls are likely to continue to provide cheaper housing and greater security of tenure than the private sector. You're normally expected to vacate halls of residence during vacations, during which time you are not responsible for rent – unlike much of the private housing available.

Halls are usually run by a warden with a democratically-elected student committee that attempts to sort out amicable solutions to some of the difficulties and charms of communal living – such as small-hour parties on one side of a desperate-to-sleep student with reggae or Mozart on the other!

Head tenancies

Colleges without adequate halls of residence may offer a second-best alternative in which they lease property directly from landlords * and then sublet to students. The college controls the lettings and acts as landlord to the students while responsible to the landlord as 'head tenant'. The students have the security of the college behind them but the landlord retains the right of guaranteed vacant possession according to the specific lease with the college. Prices of head tenancy lets are usually somewhere between halls and full market rents.

Private-rented housing
For students unable to obtain a place in hall for their first or subsequent years, the remaining choice lies in the private-rented sector. The announced intention behind the 1989 Housing Act is to increase the stock of rented housing – which has steadily diminished over the years. That intention may indeed be achieved but the proposed relaxation of rent control could result in a further considerable increase in house prices, affecting all traditional users of this type of property – the young, the single and the less-financially secure.

The quality and price of private housing varies enormously both between city centres and suburbs and between different geographical areas. The further the accommodation is from college, the cheaper it's likely to be. But travel costs have then to be taken into account. Because of the disparity in quality – and despite the housing shortage – it's vital to inspect property first before paying any advanced deposits.

The high cost of private housing in a contracting market is a crucial factor in considering the consequences for student well-being. The search is usually hard enough in itself but many students will also have to compromise their standards. If you're away from home for the first time, you may well feel lonely and unhappy – a major contributory factor in student depression and withdrawal from college. The college student counselling services are well-experienced in such matters and can be very supportive.

Where to find private housing
Most college accommodation offices produce lists of private landlords and landladies, updated regularly throughout the academic year. Local newspapers, noticeboards, shop windows and word of mouth can also be useful as sources of information.

Speed is of the essence when following up newspaper advertisements. Go for the early editions and be ready to act immediately. Beware of the subjective attitudes of landlords/landladies about your appearance, habits and origins. And don't bother to go unless you can

---

*The term 'landlord' is used here according to legal terminology and is without sexist intentions. The term 'landlady' will only be used later in relation to lodgings where meals are provided.

provide immediate deposits of at least one month's rent in advance. Because of the extreme housing shortage it's a first-come, first-served, first-secured process.

The nature of private housing
For sharing Self-contained houses/flats without landlords on the premises are usually the most popular because of relative lack of restrictions, and the ability to choose sharers. These can often be made cheaper per head by squeezing one person more than recommended into the household. However, landlords usually calculate the rent on what they consider to be reasonable use of shared facilities, which is already to their advantage. Over-crowding can create unpleasant pressures and more bad feeling within the shared household than anything else. Queuing up for the bathroom and kitchen cooker can create explosive feelings. Further potential for ill-feeling and hardship arises when the tenants are all jointly responsible for the rent but one decides to move without warning, creating a rent hardship for those who remain.

Single bedsitters Some single bedsitters have cooking facilities in the room. While the sole use of a baby cooker or gas ring has certain advantages, its use can create lingering smells in the only living space, and may also present a fire risk. Other bedsitters share cooking facilities and bathroom with other students or members of the public, not chosen by you. Disadvantages include the fact that you have no control over other tenants and the consequences of their habits. Advantages include the fact that you are not responsible for their rents if they leave and that you have a clearly-defined personal space, however small.

Landlords of private accommodation may expect rents paid throughout the vacations even if you're not resident. Others may require a retainer or reduced rent instead.

Lodgings/digs These are generally unpopular with most students because of cost, set meal times and general restrictions – such as the number of baths allowed – and the times by which you are expected to be home and in bed! Very few students now choose to adopt a well-meaning motherly landlady or a battleaxe with inflexible house-rules. Many students choose a college some way from home precisely to get away from such domestic restrictions. This also provides a convenient and acceptable way of avoiding adolescent friction with parents. Some students, nevertheless, prefer this type of accommodation because it is often more homely than college hall.

Council accommodation
Some local authorities have unlettable, poor standard or high-rise

property considered unsuitable for family households, which they may be prepared to let to students. When councils have the money to refurbish such property they then have the power to end your tenancy. Such accommodation is likely to be withdrawn as councils increasingly sell off property to private developers. Again, other homeless people from the council waiting list may be offered such property, however inadequate, as an alternative to 'bed and breakfast' accommodation. But it's always worth checking with local councils and your college for possible vacant housing of this sort.

Some mature students with children or families, already occupying council accommodation elsewhere, may wish to explore the possibility of council-property exchange through their local authority, for the duration of their course, or permanently. It's important not to lose your security of tenure in council accommodation – which is so hard to come by in the first place – by making yourself 'voluntarily homeless'. Such may be the consequence of subletting council property without prior approval of the local authority, in order to live closer to college.

The 1989 Housing Act is likely to increase insecurity of council property as well as private property. Absence from property, rent arrears and unapproved subletting will put tenants at considerable risk of eviction.

Accommodation agencies

These differ from college accommodation services in that they act not for the prospective tenant but on behalf of the landlords by pre-sifting applicants. Some agencies are explicit that they do not deal with properties below a certain rent level, while others discriminate against students or other groups. Using an agency can be expensive because the fees they charge, over and above the rent, are usually equivalent to one or two weeks' rent, plus a substantial deposit. Some disreputable agencies try to charge just for putting your name on their lists although this is illegal. *It's therefore wise to check out agency reputation, charges and terms before paying out any money.*

Hostels

Run on commercial lines or by organizations like housing associations, the YMCA or religious denominations, the best of these are as good if not better than college halls of residence. Others are very different in quality, sometimes requiring up to six people to share a room. Most provide meals. Hostels, like halls of residence, which cater for single people unable to find single accommodation, are normally over-subscribed and operate waiting lists. Your college accommodation office should be able to advise about local availability, conditions, etc.

Squatting
If all else fails, you may be forced to squat in unoccupied property. This is not to be recommended for reasons of comfort, security and the complication of getting supplies of gas, electricity, etc. But squatting itself is not illegal if you go about it the right way. Before considering squatting, you should obtain legal and practical advice either from your college accommodation office, the citizens advice bureau or the Advisory Service for Squatters (2 St Paul's Road, London, N1). The latter also publishes an excellent and comprehensive *Squatters' Handbook*.

WARNING CHECKLIST FOR ALL PRIVATE-SECTOR ACCOMMODATION

1. Don't pay any money without a receipt stating explicitly what you've paid for.
2. Find out whether deposits are returnable – and under what conditions.
3. Try to get a rent book.
4. Check whether full rent or a retainer is required during vacations.
5. Do you have exclusive/shared use of kitchen, bathroom, loo, etc.?
6. Who is responsible for damage to property, repairs, redecorations?
7. Is there a furniture inventory?
8. What security of tenure do you have?
9. In a shared property, is the tenancy jointly held or are residents individual licensees?
10. How much notice is required on either side to terminate the tenancy agreement?
11. Are the costs of heating and hot water inclusive or exclusive?
12. Are there any rules about sharers, keys, hours, etc.?
13. Is it your responsibility to provide linen, blankets, cooking utensils, etc.?
14. If you are required to sign contracts, take them first for checking to the college accommodation office or the citizens advice bureau.

ADVANTAGES AND DISADVANTAGES OF EACH

Discrimination
Some landlords welcome students from overseas because of the

possibility of high rents and limited tenancy periods. Agencies and landlords are not legally allowed to discriminate on grounds of race but ways are invariably found around this. Owners are allowed to discriminate when they live on the premises and share facilities such as the kitchen and bathroom with the tenants. Similarly, boarding houses with no more than six tenants are allowed to discriminate.

We still hear of black students who make telephone appointments to view property, only to be told it's already gone when they arrive to view. Such attitudes are hard to shift even though discrimination in housing is illegal under the race relations legislation.

Others discriminate against students on grounds of sexual orientation when they suspect them of being gay or lesbian; others on class or a whole range of subjective, stereotypical responses to the unfamiliar. Many of these types of discrimination are illegal but again they're hard to prove.

Harassment

Landlords sometimes use subtle forms of harassment to force tenants to move, such as refusal to implement vital repairs, unreasonable service charges, cutting off the telephone, etc. Others harass by invasion of privacy, with unreasonable entry into the property or even into individual rooms, on a variety of pretexts. Female students are particularly prone to sexual harassment by both landlords and other tenants. In such cases, there should be no hesitation in calling the police immediately, to prevent escalation of such difficulties.

Help with high rents – and Housing Benefit

Prices, already escalating, are likely to become even more prohibitive with the 1989 Housing Act. Water rates and 20-per-cent local-authority rates may be passed on to the student as a result of the Social Security Act 1988 and the proposed Community Charge is also likely to increase rents still further.

How can students cope with the limited resources at their command? To some extent, students are worse off financially with regard to housing costs than people on Income Support who are automatically entitled to Housing Benefit. The student grant, equivalent only to low-income-level subsistence (even if the parent or spouse pays their full calculated contribution), does not attract the same right to Housing Benefit. In calculating the amount of Housing Benefit, regulations stipulate that it must be assumed that the student is in receipt of the full grant.

Whilst the student grant contains a fixed amount for housing, it is generally regarded as well below market rates that, of course, vary according to area. That element within the grant is currently £17.80 per week in London (summer, 1988). Eligibility for Housing Benefit only begins, therefore, for that portion of the rent that exceeds the housing element with the grant.

A student in college accommodation (halls of residence and probably head tenancies because of possible subsidies) has no right to Housing Benefit other than in the summer vacation. This is because the housing element within the grant is calculated for the duration of the academic year (continuous from beginning of autumn term until the end of the academic year).

Those students resident in private accommodation can claim Housing Benefit during the period of study, but only for that element of rent that exceeds the grant contribution. So the amount of Housing Benefit is likely to be very small.

Few private tenants in the past have appealed against rent levels for fear of landlord harassment and eviction but the limited controls on rent that currently exist are likely to lessen still further when the Housing Act takes effect. However bad a landlord, there is a crucial rule that needs to be kept in mind if you don't want to put yourself on the wrong side of the law. *Never withhold rent. Argue, take advice – whatever – but rent arrears are a certain route to eviction.* With the 1989 Housing Act in effect, this will be even more strongly enforced than at present.

Because private accommodation is usually paid a month at a time, as compared to a term in advance in halls of residence, it's often tempting to lull oneself into a false sense of secure finances, spending money that should have been put aside for the rent. Remember that landlords and landladies are less tolerant of rent arrears than college authorities and you may be putting your tenancy at risk if you fall behind with the rent.

With the possibility of the whole structure of student finance changing from grants to part or full loans, entitlement to Housing Benefit may vary – possibly increasing eligibility to Housing Benefit. Legislation on that, however, is still in the future.

One thing is certain. Rents are already high and going higher. Students suffer considerable hardship as a result. Many a student has found the route to vegetarianism via depleted funds. The communal rice-pot tends to get fewer and less-exotic additions as the grant dwindles. Students may attempt forced economies on diet or take up casual part-time employment to balance their budgets, but you will have to assess for yourself the degree to which these actions may detract from your physical well-being and ability to study (see also Chapter 15 on fit for studying). Here again, student counsellors in college may help in talking you through such problems.

Security of tenure

This varies with the type of tenancy, but in all private lettings other than those where meals are provided, the tenant normally has protected tenure. The nature of that protection will depend on whether you've undertaken a holiday let, a licence or a fixed-term agreement. Many landlords try to get round the law by letting under one of these headings because of the degree of control they can exercise over the duration of the tenancy and over individual tenants. Students with individual licences within a shared tenancy, for example, have no control over the landlord's choice of other tenants with whom they may be forced to share.

But distinctions between the definitions of tenancies and licence are unclear and need to be clarified legally. Such tenancy agreements may be redefined under the 1989 Housing Act. Consult your accommodation office for further help with individual contracts before putting your signature to them.

Notice to quit

Landlords are normally required to give twenty-eight days' written notice to quit. Landladies of lodgings can ask you to go sooner. Legislation on this subject is likely to change for all new tenancies under the 1989 Housing Act. So watch out!

Security

Your personal belongings may be frugal and of little extrinsic value, but when they are lost or stolen, the cost of replacement can be surprisingly high and the distress caused may be considerable. Many students arrive at college with a new hi-fi, camera, radio, etc., which are cherished possessions. But because of communal living in halls of residence, shared housing and lodgings, it's not always possible to prevent access to your room and belongings. So, again, watch out!

Some students provide their own padlocks to rooms but the authorities or landlords may not allow this for reasons such as cleaning, safety, etc. When shared occupation is such that many people have front-door keys and some are not as careful as others about locking the front door, obvious risks occur. So it's crucial to insure your belongings from the outset. Some insurance companies have let-out clauses for those in high-risk shared occupancy, but there are some companies that specialize in students and offer reasonable terms. Your students' union will advise you. It's false economy not to have insurance on your belongings.

DO'S AND DON'TS OF SHARED LIVING

You don't know a person until you've lived with them! This is familiar, even banal, but true. The student who seems fascinating across a seminar room, or the sorrowful homesick student in the crowded bar, on whom you take pity – these are not necessarily the ones with whom it might be best to share a kitchen all year. But desperation leads people into rushed decisions when one or two people are urgently needed to make up a complement of tenants for a specific property.

Students desperate to leave home may find themselves in a worse situation than the one they left. If at all possible, it's wise to discuss attitudes to communal living before jointly moving in. In an ideal situation, flat and house sharers will have a less-anxious living space if they work out a few basic rules beforehand, which they all agree to comply with later. Here are some of the issues:

1. Rotas for house cleaning, loo disinfecting, washing up, cooker cleaning and decisions about kitty and shopping for basic shared commodities such as tea, coffee, loo paper, need to be clearly written down and displayed for all to see.
2. If and when a participant to the agreement fails to carry out one of his or her duties, will you let it ride, gripe endlessly about it or decide in advance a system of penalties?
3. Will you be cooking for yourself, communally or in turns?
4. What about laundry? Will you have a system whereby one person in turn takes the communal dirty washing to the launderette, spill it out onto a hopefully clean floor, for all to fight over whose socks are whose? Or complain because someone's red shirt has run? Or will you just do you own?
5. Who's in charge of the vegetable rack and cleaning of cupboards? Rotting carrots can poison both the atmosphere of the kitchen and the relationship.
6. How often are the cooker and the bath to be cleaned? After every use or weekly? Whose responsibility is it? Too often the role is left to a houseproud male or to the women who dig their own grave when entrapping themselves into a traditional duty, by doing it themselves out of resignation.
7. If a fond mum sends you back after a weekend at home with your favourite fruit cake, do you keep it in a tin under the bed and eat it secretly, or demolish it at one swoop by sharing it with others?

Communal living can create other strains. Those who invite friends or partners to share their rooms for short or long periods, without first discussing it with co-tenants, are bound to create resentment, let alone increased pressure on shared facilities. Despite all the rational discussions that might ideally have been held before taking on tenancies, there's nearly always one who takes liberties like this. Moreover, some sharers will change housing during the year by offering their room to another without prior discussion. The incomer might not agree to any existing house rules or feel that they can ignore them because they were not party to them initially. Once house rules break down, it's very difficult to reinstate them. Relationships are affected, quarrels erupt, studies suffer. The best remedy to all such difficulties is not to harbour grievances silently but to raise the problems as they arise and to deal with them before they get out of control.

Nevertheless, shared housing in private or college accommodation can be as educative and stimulating as the studies for which you primarily go to college. To learn how to cope in such fraught situations and to survive can be a broadening experience. However tough things might have been at home, there's usually an underlying familiarity of experience that allows family members to overcome or endure difficulties. In sharing a home with a stranger who shares no common standards of behaviour, compromises and allowances are not so easily made.

Making it work with people from different backgrounds and different cultures can be exciting and life-enhancing. When it does work, lifelong friendships can be forged with those you might never otherwise have been likely to meet. Thus, rather than re-inforcing stereotypical responses to the unfamiliar faces around, student living can be one of the most hopeful ways of breaking down prejudice.

If all this seems very technical, detailed and depressing, do not despair! There is still good accommodation to be found in most college towns and cities and not all is of the type found in the following advertisement, which recently appeared in a London evening newspaper:

> TO LET
> Desirable converted stair cupboard in Chelsea property.
> Internal fan. Share kitchen/bathroom with 4 others. Suit
> student.

A STUDENT CHECKLIST FOR FINDING ACCOMMODATION

1. Contact the college accommodation office as early as possible.
2. If the college offers first-year students priority for halls of residence, hedge your bets by applying for a place whether or not that is your first choice.
3. Consider the pros and cons of halls of residence on campus and off.
4. If your choice is, or you are forced to find, housing in the private sector, don't leave the search until the day before term commences. Consider taking a cheap base in the area before term starts from which you can study the area and the vacancies, and be ready to pounce from close at hand.
5. If you are looking for advertised vacancies in local newspapers, always buy the early edition, and follow up immediately.
6. Have plenty of coins, a phonecard and pen and paper at the ready when you begin your telephone search.
7. Make sure you have sufficient money for a month's deposit when you begin your tour of inspection.
8. Be satisfied with the answers to all the appropriate questions before parting with any money. Check first with your college accommodation office or citizens advice bureau.

SUGGESTIONS FOR FURTHER READING

Child Poverty Action Group, *National Welfare Benefits Handbook*. Details and explains recent changes in the law regarding Social Security benefits. Annually updated. Available from CPAG, 1–5 Bath Street, London EC1V 9PY.

Geoffrey Randall, *The Housing Rights Guide*. Published by SHAC, the London Housing Aid Centre, 189a Old Brompton Road, London SW5 0AR. New edition due January 1989 will detail effects of new Housing Act.

National Union of Students, *NUS Welfare Manual*. Produced annually by NUS, Nelson Mandela House, 461 Holloway Road, London N7 6LJ.

CHAR: The Housing Campaign for Single People 5–15 Cromer St. London WC1H 8LS. Various publications.

3 Students, teachers and other college staff

There is perhaps something to be said for the continued use of the term student from the motives that led the Greeks to call the Furies the Eumenides, 'the kindly ones', in the hope that the use of a flattering name might induce them to live up to it.

G.L. Brooks, *The Modern University* (1965)

This chapter tries to do three things:

1. To help you relate to your fellow students.
2. To help you understand college teachers better.
3. To tell you something about the work of other college staff.

STUDENTS: IT TAKES ALL KINDS

In your first days at college, you'll rub shoulders with many other students – and you won't always find it easy to relate to them. Who are all these shy/brash, so much younger/older, so much brighter/duller, so much better/worse-dressed students? How do you relate to them?

Let's look at some typical groups of college students in Britain. In earlier decades – say, from the 1950s to the 1970s – most but not all college students were secondary school-leavers – now called 'traditional students' because they arrive at college via the traditional route from school. But there was nearly always a small group of so-called 'mature students', who had failed to get to college when they left school (due to illness, perhaps, or economic circumstances or the disruption caused by the Second World War of 1939–45). Today there are many more such 'mature students'. What are they doing at college in their thirties and forties – or even their fifties?

Very few colleges these days refuse admission on grounds of age alone. Entry is normally open to all who can demonstrate a capacity to keep up with the courses and to benefit from such study, regardless of age or background. College was never designed exclusively for younger students – though they generally constitute the largest single group.

Colleges welcome mature students for two reasons. First, because human curiosity is insatiable. The capacity for intellectual and psychological growth through learning goes on throughout life. Mature students bring their whole life experience to college, they have potentially much to gain – and, therefore, much to offer the communities to which they return after college. The age barriers to college entry are now rapidly crumbling, giving place to a policy of 'open access' – which means college admission to students of all ages who can demonstrate their capacity to benefit from study.

Second, the majority of those studying at British colleges are so-called 'home students', which includes students from other European countries (or more accurately, from countries within the membership of the European Economic Community). But there are nearly always some overseas students – mostly from Africa or Asia but including some from America or even Australasia. What are they doing here? Some will be privately funded (i.e. paying their own way or grant aided by independent foundations). Some will be scholarship holders, sent abroad to study by their own governments in order to increase the supply of educated, trained and skilled people in their home economies. For that reason, the majority are likely to be studying technical or vocational subjects that equip them with more immediately useful skills. Others will be following more conventional, academic types of college courses.

Another general observation worth making is that, whereas in the past the majority of students at British colleges were likely to be male (except perhaps on specialized vocational courses such as fashion design, hairdressing or nursing), higher and further education in Britain now attracts almost equal numbers of men and women students. The admission policy of most colleges reflects the rough numerical balance of men and women in the wider community. Although this means that student groups are more evenly balanced by gender than was the case with earlier generations of students, men still outnumber women in so-called 'traditional' male subjects such as maths, engineering and applied science. (See the annual reports of the Equal Opportunities Commission, the body responsible for promoting equality between the sexes, which monitors and analyses the proportion of men and women entering higher and further education courses.)

Whether they are men or women, from home or overseas, of the traditional or mature variety, students conform to no single model but reflect the widest variety of human types. Don't imagine for one moment that most college students are intellectual 'egg-heads' – and that you are the exception. In any representative sample of students, there will be a statistically small number of highly intelligent students. Most students, by definition, will be of average ability, with a smaller number below average. But assessed differences in the abilities of students at college admission are notoriously unreliable predictors to performance because so much depends on personality, on character and on 'intelligence in action' – that is, the active use to which students put their intellectual capacities.

So, be prepared for some close encounters with interesting students of all kinds. But don't expect your fellow students to constitute a representative cross-section of the community at large – if only because they contain an above-average proportion of younger people and others who are most able to sustain continuous study and to benefit from college education.

WHAT ABOUT COLLEGE TEACHERS? ARE THEY REALLY HUMAN?

An Academic

You sit at your fat desk, starching
your brains: you're the tone-deaf man
in the orchestra, you're the frog
who wouldn't a-wooing go.

What a job is this, to measure
lightning with a footrule, the heart's
turbulence with a pair of callipers.
And what a magician who can

dismantle Juliet, Ahab, Agamemnon
into a do-it-yourself kit
of semantic gestures.

Tidiness is decent. Trains
have to reach their destinations.
But yours, that should be
clattering and singing
through villages and landscapes, never
gets out of the shunting yards.

I'm a simple man – I believe
you were born, I believe it
against all the evidence.
I would like to give you
a present of weather, a
transfusion of pain.

Norman MacCaig *Collected Poems* (1985)

Because they lead somewhat unusual lives, college teachers are often subjected to this type of elaborate caricature. The popular image of the absent-minded, long-haired professor may have given way in recent years to the well-suited, urbane telly-don, but college teachers are still often represented as colourful, eccentric and even controversial figures: exotic creatures, trapped in a forlorn struggle between an unfeeling college bureaucracy on the one hand and an unthinking – nay, an invincible – student ignorance on the other.

The reality is less dramatic, more complex, more fascinating. College teachers comprise a richly-varied tribe. Think, for example, of the ineffectual Oxbridge dons portrayed by Evelyn Waugh in *Brideshead Revisited*; the miscreant, Welsh, history teacher, Jim Dixon, in Kingsley Amis's *Lucky Jim*; the snooty but endearing Professor Higgins in George Bernard Shaw's *Pygmalion*, transferred to the screen as *My Fair Lady*; Albert Corde, the Chicago college dean, stranded in Bucharest, in Saul Bellow's *The Dean's December*; Henry Wilt, the polytechnic English lecturer, dinning 'Eng. Lit' into the unreceptive skulls of rude mechanicals in Tom Sharpe's *Wilt*; Dr Petworth, the luckless linguist in Malcolm Bradbury's *Rates of Exchange* – a practised cultural traveller – an academic like Norman MacCaig's – styleless, white and male, forty and married, bourgeois and British. Or the British academic, Philip Swallow and his American counterpart, Morris Zapp, in David Lodge's *Changing Places* – 'academics on the move, in the air, on the make' – who have exchanged the plate-glass, concrete jungle of Euphoria State University, USA, for the damp, red-brick University of Rummidge, UK; or the unworldly dons of the 1987 television series, *Porterhouse Blue*.

One explanation for all this brilliant caricaturing of college teachers might be that they really are larger than life, as portrayed. Or could it simply be that many of our best satirical writers were themselves college lecturers? After all, not many business executives or lawyers write satirical novels or plays about their own profession. (John Mortimer may be the exception that proves the rule.)

Apart from a small number of mature entrants to the profession, most college teachers are drawn direct from the ranks of successful former students. This does not mean that they are all eminent scholars (a term reserved for a handful of rare spirits – like Albert Einstein, Bertrand Russell and others – who have shattered the frontiers of human knowledge, earning world-wide distinction by their intellectual endeavours). Most college teachers are more down-to-earth: solid citizens and safe, intellectual craft workers, who mostly know and love their subject well enough to wish to share their enthusiasm for it with their students.

Every college teacher in Britain will be a graduate and most will have acquired some higher qualification (e.g. a master's degree or a doctorate of philosophy) by extended study and examination. But this does not necessarily or even generally mean that every college teacher can teach. Few will have attended a course in pedagogy – the art and science of educational methods. A few college teachers are undoubtedly brilliant exponents of their subject. Others may be outstanding researchers or prolific academic authors. But you should not assume that college teachers are all professionally-trained teachers. Experience will quickly show they're not!

College teachers may have unusual contracts of employment that means they often work irregular hours. Everybody knows that college teachers have long holidays, but few people appreciate the variety or intensity of the demands made on college teachers. In addition to their normal teaching duties, many college teachers will teach evening-class students, which means they may not be back at college until late the following day. Nearly all college teachers also have a contractual obligation to research and to publish; to carry their share of departmental and/or college administration; to serve on college committees and other policy-making or advisory bodies; to set and to mark college examinations; to be available to help students whenever possible; and so on.

Because they live busy academic lives, college teachers are not always available just when you want to see them. Many teachers display a notice outside their college doors, advising students of their regular hours for 'consultation without appointment'. Others will normally have made arrangements with the departmental secretary for seeing students by appointment. If you chance to meet your college teachers when crossing the campus but they don't stop to talk to you, don't take offence. They are quite likely to be moving rapidly from one lecture hall to another in consecutive hours. So, please don't assume that teachers have nothing else to do but give lectures and await your arrival in their rooms.

A few other things are worth noting about the life-style of college teachers. They tend to dress for comfort and convenience rather than to impress. At Oxbridge and some other colleges, teaching staff may wear academic gowns (though not academic headgear, except at ceremonial occasions). At other colleges, some professors and other senior (i.e. better-paid) academic staff may wear collars and ties with more formal suits. But the majority of college teachers, both men and women, dress informally, in keeping with long-standing academic tradition.

Academic staff are voracious readers and inveterate talkers. This helps them to keep up with their subject and sometimes with their colleagues. They are often to be seen engaged in passionate argument and vociferous debate. This is the very stuff of college life. It takes place all the time and should not be confused with organizational politicking (which generally takes place behind closed doors) or personal vituperation (which generally takes place in committee rooms).

With the academic thirst for knowledge goes the academic's well-publicized thirst for alcoholic refreshment. This is hardly surprising amongst members of a profession who earn a good deal of their living by talking. But alcoholism is a lesser occupational hazard amongst academics than it is amongst, say, media people, advertising agents or lawyers. The appreciation of fine wine and the appreciation of fine intellectual distinctions often go together. And because they are mostly sociable creatures, academics enjoy slaking their thirst in the senior common room, in campus bars and off-campus pubs. They will be seen partaking of hospitality at college wine-and-cheese parties, at welcoming sherry receptions, at meetings of convocation and examination boards, at end-of-term wind-up parties and graduation celebrations.

However, the fact that students and academics share a taste for informal dress and for the occasional drink should not mislead you into thinking that students and academic staff are equals. That's an unwarranted assumption – for all college teachers are in a position of academic authority. That's to say, as well as teaching and helping students learn, college teachers may also have some formal responsibility for student behaviour and discipline. So, whilst they may encourage an atmosphere of informal comradeship and sociable learning, college teachers are not your equals and you should not expect them to treat you as such. If in doubt, play safe – at least initially. Use first names only when invited to do so.

OTHER COLLEGE STAFF: WHAT DO THEY DO?

> *First come I; my name is Jowett.*
> *There's no knowledge but I know it.*
> *I am the Master of the College.*
> *What I don't know isn't knowledge.*
> H.C. Beeching, *The Masque of Balliol*

Besides college teachers, you'll come into contact with some other important members of college staff. It's worth knowing who they are and what they do. Let's make our way through the organization chart of an imaginary college.

At the top, there's the university vice-chancellor (principal, director or master in the case of a college). He or she is the chief executive with overall responsibility for running the institution. In most universities, he or she is often called the vice-chancellor – the title 'chancellor' being reserved for another notable figure who fills that largely ceremonial and dignified office. (Note that most heads of colleges and vice-chancellors in Britain are still men – even though chancellors include some very distinguished women.)

The typical British college head is supported by a team comprising several principal officers:

1. *The academic registrar* The academic registrar is a full-time administrator, responsible for all matters academic – from the appointment of academic staff to the admission of students, from college statutes and rules to formal relationships between the college and its principal funding authorities.

    The academic registrar is normally a legally-qualified person who advises the principal at meetings of the major academic decision-making body (sometimes called 'senate'). Overall responsibility for college policy usually rests with the college court.

2. *The bursar* The bursar is another full-time administrator, responsible for all matters relating to college funding and the control of college financial expenditures. The bursar's staff normally administer academic and other staff salaries as well as student grants and loans.

    Bursars these days wear permanently-worried expressions because they are chiefly pre-occupied with the financial income and expenditure. With current British government policy of reduced funding for colleges of higher and further education, the bursar's staff spend much of their time these days in trying to find ways of balancing the college's books by reducing overspending in order to restore financial viability and so preserve college existence.

3. *The librarian* The librarian is what might today be called the college's chief information scientist – responsible for the policy and running of one of the college's principal physical assets – its information base, contained in books, journals, computer and microfiche stores and archives.

   With the phenomenal explosion of information science in recent years, the vast increase in publishing costs and the reduction in government grants to educational establishments, librarians seem to spend a great deal of their time these days poring over computer print-outs on library utilization, in order to help them decide where to recommend cutbacks in library service (e.g. shorter opening hours or reduced service from enquiry desks).

4. *Deans* At collegiate institutions, like Oxbridge, colleges normally appoint a dean of undergraduates, responsible for carrying out college policy on all matters relating to undergraduates. At other, more unified institutions, both universities and polytechnics, the dean will be the person with overall responsibility for administration within a particular faculty (e.g. science, engineering, arts and social studies, business, and so on).

Each of these principal officers will have a deputy (e.g. vice-dean) and a group of qualified staff specialists to help them administer college affairs. Whether or not you think you'll ever need to use their services (see Chapter 21 on where to go for advice and help), it's important to get to know who they are and what they do.

For example, the librarian will certainly have qualified and trained staff to help you get the best out of the library's resources (see Chapter 8 on more effective reading). Then there's usually a student (or undergraduate) registry that looks after college admissions, examinations, records, timetables and so on. Sooner or later, you'll be paying them a visit (see Chapter 4 on choosing subjects and class options). Then there's the student advisory service or welfare office (names vary from college to college), responsible for helping students with a range of services from accommodation (see Chapter 2 on accommodation) and student health (see Chapter 18 on managing stress) to careers counselling (see Chapter 22 on career choice and job search) and alumni relations (see the final chapter, So, what did you get out of college?).

Finally, it's worth noting that most colleges have an extensive range of services offered by the college or student union. These are run independently of college authorities (although they may be supported and encouraged by them). So, if you need a sympathetic ear or advice on a problem you've failed to resolve with the relevant college office, it will often pay you to consult the student-union Office.

SUGGESTIONS FOR FURTHER READING

A.H. Halsey and M. Trow: *The British Academic*, London: Faber, 1971.
J.N. Gardner and A.J. Jewler: *College is only the Beginning*, Belmont, CA: Wadsworth, 1985, Ch. 3 'Decoding your Professors'

4 Choosing subjects and class options

*'I didn't take any history in college,' said the sweet girl
graduate. 'I took "Social Mal" instead.'*
I beg your pardon?
*'Oh, sorry, that's what we called a course in Social
Maladjustment that Professor X gave.'*
You mean you have learned maladjustment?
*'Yes, the causes of it. You know – inhibitions,
divorce, and all that sort of thing.'*
*I see. And now you want to take History, get a higher
degree, and ultimately teach?*
Jacques Barzun, *We Who Teach* (1944)

This chapter tries to do three things:

1. To examine the reasons for studying a particular subject.
2. To discuss the choice of academic subjects.
3. To suggest how best to make your class options.

REASONS FOR STUDYING PARTICULAR SUBJECTS

There are at least three good reasons for choosing to study a subject at college:

1. Because you find the subject inherently interesting and therefore want to know more about it. This often means that you've studied the subject at a lower level before coming to college – and have done reasonably well at it. But you should *not* simply stick to subjects in which you did well at school. Consider the whole range.
2. Because the subject deals with some important aspects of the society in which you live and work and hope to earn your living. It pays to equip yourself with an understanding of a society that will change so much in political, economic, social, scientific, technological and cultural terms during your own working lifetime. The relevance of an academic subject to the non-academic, outside world is a useful guideline.
3. Because the subject is practically useful and will stand you in good stead when you set out on your chosen career. 'Vocational' subjects – like medicine, engineering, law or accountancy – prepare students more directly for their first jobs. Other subjects – like maths, economics, material sciences or history – are less career-oriented and allow you more freedom to choose your career as your interests develop and labour markets change. Finally, there are those subjects – like English, history and philosophy – which provide critical intellectual training of a kind that will prove invaluable, whatever you choose to do with the rest of your life.

HOW DO YOU CHOOSE WHICH SUBJECTS TO STUDY?

The first point is that you can't make a meaningful choice of subjects without adequate information. If you're not sure which subjects to study, seek further information from the college registry or the subject department itself. College staff are used to explaining their subjects to students, especially at the start of each academic session. Many colleges organize an 'electives fair' at which students are given a broad general introduction to subjects on offer during that session.

The second point is that you should certainly select subjects you think you will enjoy. Consult your personal preferences and established interests. Ask yourself two questions:

1. Do I already know enough about this subject, as taught at this college? The approach might be quite different from what you suppose. Don't engage in self-deception. Find out more before making your final choice.
2. From what I already know, will I enjoy studying the subject for one, two or possibly more years? If you devote several years of your life to a subject, you ought to be reasonably sure that you'll enjoy it. And you'll certainly do better at subjects you enjoy, rather than those you feel you ought to do or are required to do.

The third point is to consider choosing subjects that help you make sense of your own society. Most colleges offer a range of subjects that examine society from a critical and constructive viewpoint. You are encouraged to question the world as it is and to ask how it might be better organized to meet individual and social needs and wants. College students in the 1990s should have their eyes firmly fixed on the year 2000 and beyond. Therefore, consider how your choice of subjects might help you prepare yourself for survival and success in the world of the twenty-first century.

The fourth point is to check whether your choice of a particular subject calls for any prior knowledge or qualification; or whether it carries with it the obligation to study a related subject. For example, you may not be allowed to study, say, economics unless you also take statistics or computing. Or there may be a prescribed test of mathematics before you can proceed to advanced mathematics, or a prescribed standard of attainment in maths before you can begin electrical engineering.

The fifth point is that you should keep an open mind about your choice of subjects and be willing to change your subject choice before you become too emotionally committed. Most colleges will allow students to change their subject choices in the early weeks of an academic session. Thereafter, you may find it very difficult or impossible to change – because you will by then have missed so much of the introductory lectures and classes. If in doubt, keep two provisional subjects going for the first half of the first term – and then drop the one that appeals to you the less.

HOW TO CHOOSE YOUR CLASS OPTIONS

When you've decided your field of study, you still need to make your class options (always assuming you're allowed any choice). 'Electives', as they're sometimes called, enable you to narrow your focus of study onto those specific subjects/classes that interest you the most. For example, if you were a first-year student at the University of Strathclyde Business School in Glasgow, Scotland, you would have a very wide range of class options within the first year of your BA degree course. The BA pass degree consists of thirteen classes (or their equivalent) taken over three years – five classes taken in the first year and usually four in each of the following two years. Alternatively, it's possible to accumulate credits from each of the class options you choose. Each class is given a credit rating (normally one credit per class, but some half-classes like Quantitative Methods or Computing, which are obligatory in the Business School, may carry only a half credit). You'd then be able to choose between, say, Economics I, Business Law I, Accounting I, Industrial Relations I and so on. The way you decide how to exercise your class options is by reading the class syllabus, published in the college prospectus (or undergraduate handbook), discussing the relative attractiveness and utility of the classes (and their teachers!) with second-year students, or your adviser of studies or with the teachers themselves – or with a combination of all these.

Most colleges have now gone over to the modular system of teaching, which means you can achieve your degree (or other qualification) by combining the study of those subjects, however dissimilar, which interest you the most. Thus, you may take mathematics with music or politics with personnel management – both attractive combinations!

It cannot be too highly stressed that nobody else can exercise your subject/class choice but you. It therefore pays to make the earliest and fullest possible enquiries before exercising your option choice. In that way, you minimize the risk of making a poor choice and a false start in your first year, with the consequent possibility of having to catch up by taking extra classes or to repeat classes the following year.

SUGGESTIONS FOR FURTHER READING

Association of Commonwealth Universities: *University Entrance*, London: Association of Commonwealth Universities, annually
CRAC: *Degree Course Guides*, Cambridge: CRAC, annually
Your College Study Guide/Handbook
Your Faculty Study Guides and Departmental Course Curricula

5 Managing your time at college

*After rising and saying his prayers, the poet should
retire to his study and . . . engage in the study of the
ancillary sciences: lexicography, metrics and so forth
. . . The second quarter of the day should be devoted to
poetic composition . . . Then, in the last part of the day,
he should revise what he has composed in the morning
. . . After evening prayers, a fair copy should be made
of the day's composition . . . The second and third
quarters of the night are to be devoted to sleep.*
  Raja-Shikara, *Prescription for the Way of Life a Poet
      should Follow* (tenth century AD)

This chapter tries to do three things:

1. To introduce the concept of time management.
2. To help you practise better time management.
3. To suggest some useful points in managing time.

THE CONCEPT OF TIME MANAGEMENT

The secret of survival and success at college can be very largely defined in terms of how well you organize your time. In schools, factories and workshops, somebody else prescribes how you should spend your time – and checks that you don't abuse the timetable. At college, the responsibility for how you use your time is handed back to you. You become, to that extent, a potentially more autonomous individual. You have much greater freedom of choice how you spend your time – but that freedom also confers greater responsibility on you.

Survival means continuity through time . . . and success means making the best of your opportunities within a given time-frame. You can't succeed if you don't survive. So, survival needs come first. What are those needs? How do they fit into our total human needs, in rough order, from lower to higher order needs? (Note that we speak here of needs, not wants!)

1. Oxygen – without which we quickly die as living organisms.
2. Food and drink – without which our bodies soon lose their efficiency.
3. Warmth and shelter – without which we feel uncomfortable and distressed.
4. Human society – without which we remain atomistic individuals, isolated and alone.
5. Physical activity – without which we feel deprived of our most human attributes.
6. Mental stimulation – of which college studying should provide an abundance.

Given that these survival needs are common to all humans, we vary greatly in the quantity and timing of those needs. Some of us have a lower threshold of boredom; some have a better physical metabolism; others have a lower resistance to cold; and so on. The time we spend attending to these individual needs is bound to vary somewhat. That's why it's impossible to be prescriptive about how you should allocate your own time – and that's why it's essential that you learn how best to manage your time for yourself.

HOW TO PRACTISE BETTER TIME MANAGEMENT

Time as a scarce resource

You need to come to terms with the fact that whilst time is objectively finite and inelastic, you know from personal experience that time can seem highly elastic. Think how time flies in periods of intense, purposeful activity. Then compare periods of skull-numbing, unrewarding boredom or inactivity. So, time is your most scarce and valuable resource – especially in examinations.

Getting organized

You need to organize your life if you are to make the most of your limited time at college. You'll find certain external time demands are made on you. For example, you must attend certain lectures and tutorials; you must present assignments by prescribed dates; you must complete a course of study within a given number of years. Those external demands provide a time-frame within which you must organize the rest of your activities and focus your attention.

Your academic course

You should begin by focusing your attention on your academic course as a whole. How many years will it take to complete the course by full-time study? Can you switch to part-time study, if necessary? Is there a qualifying period before you can present yourself for examination? What combination of subjects is mandatory or recommended?

The academic session

You should then focus on one academic session, normally much less than a full twelve-month period. How much of your time will you devote to study during academic terms? How much will be devoted to other demands – home, family, paid employment perhaps? How will you spend the academic vacations? Not the same as holidays! This might be the best time to get that extra reading done; to work on a project report; to earn spare cash; or to attend to non-urgent domestic responsibilities.

The syllabus

Next, focus carefully on the syllabus for each class, noting key sub-divisions and the proportion of the session devoted to each. For example, if you have to undertake practical work (e.g. placement with an organization) as part of your course, who obtains that placement and how closely does it have to fit in with academic training?

The college term

Focus next on the college term (or semester). How many weeks does it comprise? What significant event(s) mark the end of that term (e.g. examinations)? You should make yourself a simple planning diary of the weeks of the term, boldly marking key weeks and dates. This planning diary should show, for example, weeks in which certain lecture courses begin or in which certain work assignments are due for presentation; weeks in which there are social or sporting events; weeks in which you are free to take a break or to go away for a few days.

SOME USEFUL POINTS IN TIME MANAGEMENT

(See Figure 4.1.)

1. You need to develop a weekly timetable, covering all your waking hours – between, say, 7 am and midnight, including weekends. Begin by deciding how many hours sleep you expect to need throughout the week. Block in those hours as sacrosanct. Remember, if you go to a late-night party, you'll need to make up those lost hours of sleep – probably at week-ends.
2. Then, block in all lecture, tutorial or seminar hours. These are hours when you know you need to be somewhere on time – so build in margins for travel.
3. Next, allow adequate times for refreshment – both meal-times and snacks and short periods of physical exercise and fresh air. It's a good idea to block in regular periods of exercise. That way you keep yourself physically fit for mental activity.
4. Finally, you are left with unallocated time which you must distribute equitably between your different subjects, in line with your known study patterns – and leisure activities. If, for example, you have two lectures a week in a particular subject – say, on Tuesday and Thursday mornings – and a weekly tutorial – say, on Tuesday afternoons – then you should set aside regular time(s) – say, an hour or two on a Monday and another hour on, say, a Thursday – to study and prepare for that class. Ditto for other classes.

Your planning diary and your weekly timetable are simply management tools – they work for you, not the other way round. In other words, by planning and timetabling, you organize your present time in order to have future time. In that way, you can take time out of timetable for that unexpected event – the party invitation or concert or visiting speaker – without disturbing your study for survival and success.

There's much more to effective time management. To succeed, you must meet your deadlines. If you fail to complete assignments on time, you may lose marks, credits, or be required to repeat some courses. A Research Dissertation which is late may result in your being unable to

Hours	Monday	Tuesday	Wednesday	Thursday	Friday	Saturday
08–09	Jogging, ablutions, breakfast Travelling time					
09–10	Study	Indl. Relns	Study	Indl. Relns	History	Shopping
10–11	Econ.	Free	History	Study	Econ.	Shopping
11–12	Study	Law	History Tutorial	Study	Free	Shopping
12–13	Lunch	Lunch	Lunch	Econ. Tutorial	Lunch	
13–14	Free	Free	Travel	Lunch	Free	Sport
14–15	Comput. Lab.	IR Tutorial	Sport	Comput. Lab.	Law	Sport
15–16	Free	Comput. Lab.	Sport	Free	Law Tutorial	Sport
16–17	Tea	Tea	Sport	Drama	Free	Sport
17–18	Music	Music	Tea	Drama	Free	
18–19	Travelling time					
19–20	Meal	Meal	Meal	Meal	Meal	
20–21	Study	Study	Study	Study	Free	
21–22	Study	Study	Study	Study	Free	

Figure 4.1   A weekly college timetable

graduate for a further year. Learn to adjust your priorities as earlier assignments are completed and new ones taken on. Don't procrastinate – make a start on each project as soon as possible.

SUGGESTIONS FOR FURTHER READING

Adair, J., *Effective Time Management*, London: Pan Books, 1982.
Haynes, M.E., *Making Every Minute Count*, London: Kogan Page, 1987.

6 Developing good study habits

I don't have to worry about waking up . . . So the day begins with a flying start . . . Then I try to do my air force exercises . . . While I'm shaving I tell myself what the opening sentence will be when I begin to write a few minutes later . . . Then I have a very light breakfast . . . go through to my study and from then on I'm not interrupted – not at all . . . There's no hesitation when I get down to work.
Wilbur Smith, 'A Life in the Day Of. . .', The Sunday Times, July 1987

This chapter tries to do three things:

1. To explain the importance of good study habits.
2. To suggest some of the best ways to study.
3. To point out what is meant by effective study.

THE IMPORTANCE OF GOOD STUDY HABITS

Human beings are said to be slaves of habit. How many of us could survive for long without some predictable pattern or regularity in our lives? Yet we also need stimulating change and variety. Habitual activity gives our lives an element of security – the daily pattern of eating, sleeping, ablution and exercise – which provides the essential framework within which we can then be adventurous, taking some risk, enjoying the stimulation of the new and exciting.

To survive and succeed as a student, you'll need to develop your own pattern of regular activity, within which you can feel secure and become an effective student, leaving yourself sufficient freedom to be spontaneous, to be yourself.

It's difficult to exaggerate the importance of developing good study habits, yet it's impossible to prescribe any one, single set of study habits for all students. The reason for this is that students are not a homogeneous category. Successful students study in a variety of different ways, most of them equally valid and effective – so it would be presumptuous or simply wrong to recommend any one proven pattern of study habits and tell all students to conform to that pattern.

Instead, we urge you to get to know which particular pattern suits your personal needs – to record, analyse and, if necessary, to adapt that pattern in ways we shall suggest – and then to stick to it. For example, if you play sport regularly – say, on Wednesday and Saturday afternoons – it's important that you eat and rest sensibly before your game, in order to be in top form and play your best. Similarly, if you have a regular tutorial at say, 11 am each Tuesday, it makes sense to set aside some part of Monday to prepare yourself for the Tuesday tutorial (see Chapter 5 on managing your time at college).

Let's assume you've worked out your timetable for the term/semester. How should you get down to your actual studies? Experience suggests there's no better recipe for successful study than regular, patterned activity. Patterns provide predictability – and predictability offers a measure of security and confidence.

WHAT'S THE BEST WAY TO STUDY?

Where you study is the first important step towards survival and success as a student. Just as you know you must be in certain lecture halls for certain regular lectures, so you need to know where you should be for other forms of study.

What you need is a quiet, reasonably warm and well-lit room and a comfortable (not too comfortable!) chair and a table or desk to work at. If you're lucky enough to live at home, or you have your own room in college or good lodgings, you may prefer to study there (see also Chapter 2 on accommodation). But most students will spend much of their time working in the college library, study centre or some other

room set aside for quiet study (i.e. *not* the refectory or student union).
Where you study matters for four reasons:

1.   You settle down more quickly in a place you know rather than a
     new place where you need time to get used to the seating, the
     lighting, the visual distractions.
2.   You associate that place with a particular set of activities, so that
     returning to that place reinforces your mental concentration and
     allows you to work better.
3.   You spend less time searching for a place to work and more time
     actually working. It's amazing how much time can be spent
     getting down to work – without actually doing any!
4.   You can be more easily found by your friends if you have a settled
     place of work. So they spend less time searching for you and more
     time in your company.

The place itself should be conducive to study without being too
comfortable. Your mental concentration is reduced by too much
physical well-being. An armchair by the fire in winter may be the ideal
spot for reading a novel: however, it's not the best place to structure or
write an essay on 'Newtonian thermodynamics' or 'Political and
philosophical influences on the novels of Jane Austen'.

You should aim to avoid every kind of distraction that takes your
mind away from your work.

Visual distraction
Visual distraction may be the easiest to contend with. Many libraries
offer study places, separated by physical dividers to cut down visual
distractions, or, better still, carrels (partly-enclosed study cells) that
cut out both visual and aural distractions. Elsewhere, choose a seat
facing a blank wall, rather than one facing a pinboard with pictures,
recipes, messages and other seductive images. A single, familiar image
(e.g. a favourite photograph) may be reassuring and even
inspirational.

Eye-strain
Eye-strain is another powerful visual distraction. There are two
sources: physical and psychological. Any form of stress may produce
headaches, eye-strain and tiredness (see Chapter 18 on managing
stress). However, the physical cause may simply be poor lighting: too
little, too much, from the wrong angle or of the wrong colour. An ideal
gift for any student is an adjustable desk lamp, the more flexible the
better. If the physical lighting is acceptable, and the eye-strain persists,
consult your medical practitioner or an ophthalmic optician. Don't
strain your eyes by putting up with poor lighting.

Noise and vibration

Noise and vibration of any kind is a powerful distraction – but words are more distracting than music. Many students say they can't work effectively without some favourite background music (this chapter is being drafted to the background of a Mozart quartet – the perfect inspiration!). Of course, that's a matter of taste. But if workmen are hammering outside your door, if the noise is intermittent and/or high-pitched, if you can't switch it off at will, you may find such noise psychologically distressing as well as distracting.

If your next-door neighbours insist on blasting you at all hours with Wagner's Göttedämmerung', be thankful: it might have been Heavy Metal. Don't retaliate. First, try reasoning with them. Then, seek the support of other students who are similarly distracted. Finally, take the matter up with the accommodation authorities (see Chapter 2 on accommodation). Don't allow noise to distract you from your work – or rob you of sound sleep. Start the way you intend to continue.

Are you sitting comfortably?

The 'fundamental' principle of education is that the head can only take what the seat can take. Your chair needs to support your spine, cushion your bottom and be at a convenient height for writing – but it does not need to be upholstered or to swivel or to have a head/footrest or whatever. Find a chair that suits your needs and stick to it. Once more, the familiar is comfortable and supportive, but don't neglect to get up and walk around the building – or better still, around the block – from time to time, to stimulate the supply of oxygen to the brain. Or try working in a standing position.

Smells and odours

Smells and odours may be the most powerful single distraction of all – especially if they're delicious cooking smells – because they're the most pervasive and difficult to deal with. If you have overseas students in the room below who cook curry at all hours, you really have only two choices: learn to enjoy curry or try to get a room change. If neither solution is practical, try burning a joss-stick or invest in a large aerosol spray.

Finally, amongst the physical prerequisites for effective study, you need a place to study that is warm without being soporific, well-ventilated without being windswept, fresh without being frozen. An air-conditioned library, laboratory or computer suite is ideal. Failing that, a large room with a high ceiling is better than a cupboard. But the most important requirement is a window that opens, with blinds or curtains that may be drawn against summer sun or winter blasts.

WHEN TO STUDY EFFECTIVELY?

When you choose to study is your own decision. How you make that decision is critical to your survival and success as a student. A student's life is ruled by the clock: there's a time to be up and about if you want breakfast; a time to be in college for a lecture or tutorial; a time by which you must hand in an essay or project report; a time to study and a time to relax.

We begin, as usual, with you – and with self-knowledge. What's your temperament and life-style? Are you a 'dawn raider' or a 'midnight cowboy'? Do you come alive slowly in the mornings or do you leap out of bed searching for a pencil to capture your best thoughts? We're all different – and yet there are some sound guidelines from which we can all learn:

1. Self-knowledge is a cardinal virtue. Students are often slow to recognize their own best study times. We need to think about ourselves as well-functioning organisms without becoming too self-conscious, inhibited or paralyzed by morbid introspection.
2. A few students find they think more clearly and creatively after early morning tea/coffee and before breakfast. Others need to raise their blood sugar levels before they get any ideas. Some of us are more mentally productive before midday; others only come to life in the second half of the day. Still others do their best work when most of us have gone to sleep.
3. Just as there's no one best study pattern for all students, so there are no set times of the day for different types of study. Skimming a chapter for its main ideas may be done over coffee. Structuring a complex essay may demand total, uninterrupted concentration for an hour or more before lunch. Taking notes in the library may be spread over an afternoon.
4. Get to know when you are at your best for different types of study and try to do them when you know you're at your best. Your work won't always fit into these ideal time slots, but at least you'll know why you're less productive at other times.
5. Watch out for tell-tale signs of fatigue and stress. There will be times when you simply can't work effectively at all. In that case, you might as well pack up your books and take some moderately energetic exercise – which is usually more therapeutic than brooding over your mental blockage.
6. Try to increase your attention span and extend the length of time over which you can work effectively. Study your own body chemistry. Discover how and when and why you tire physically and mentally. Most healthy adults in the West seem to require

food at four-hourly intervals and fluid refreshment at two-hourly intervals. But there are considerable individual variations. Find out how often your own body needs to replenish its energy stores. And pay closer attention to understanding what your body is telling you about yourself.

WHAT IS EFFECTIVE STUDY?

Efficiency (or productivity) is an economic concept – a measure of relative outputs for given inputs, of time or energy or effort. Effectiveness, by contrast, is not about relative performance but about achieving pre-set targets or objectives. Effective study does not mean reading twice as fast (one measure of efficiency) or writing twice as much in a given time period (another measure of output over input). Effective study implies some deeper reflection about overall educational objectives as well as the structure and content of human learning.

Research evidence shows that, whilst human adults vary greatly in their intellectual curiosity and their levels of mental energy, most of us learn by the unconscious process of internalizing knowledge, skills or attitudes that have a more-or-less permanent effect on our subsequent behaviour. Of course, we may forget old lessons and we certainly need to keep in practice to maintain our performance levels in certain types of skill (especially psycho-motor skills – like playing a musical instrument or carrying out a laboratory procedure). Research evidence also shows that learning is of two qualitatively different kinds:

1. Shallow or superficial learning – like learning a name, address and telephone number that you promptly forget unless you write them down or consciously commit them to memory or use them habitually.
2. Deep learning – like knowing how to dress yourself or clean your teeth or ride a bicycle, which you learned to do when young and which have entered your consciousness at a deeper level so that you rarely think consciously about them because you engage in these activities daily and apparently intuitively.

All too often, students engage in study that only results in shallow or superficial learning of the first type – for example, the rote learning of names, dates, superficial factual data and characteristics that you hold in your short-term memory just long enough to pass an examination and that are then rapidly forgotten, because they have not been internalized – perhaps because our psyches know they are not of much use in the long run. Our psyches are simply refusing to be overloaded.

Deep learning, on the other hand, is the kind you take with you through the rest of your life: like Paul of Tarsus's conversion on the road to Damascus, or the kind of insights vouchsafed to Jean-Jacques Rousseau when he fell asleep under his tree of knowledge. When you know something like that, you have absorbed it so deeply into your consciousness that it is never likely to be displaced, except perhaps by brain-washing or frontal lobotomy.

Priorities

Priorities are your next task. You must keep up with the full range of your subjects – but where do you begin? There's always a strong temptation to put off the most difficult task or the least congenial subject. Resist that temptation by turning it on its head. Tackle your most difficult assignments first! You must avoid negative study habits – like telling yourself you'll begin that essay when you've taken notes from one more book. And then, just one more. Begin to structure your ideas today – and then decide whether you need to do more reading.

Make a start!

Once you've settled you priorities, don't keep finding reasons (i.e. excuses) for not starting just yet. There's nearly always something else you could do, rather than study. Try making a 'clean start' – say, on the hour – and don't give up until you've completed a reasonable work stint. Regular breaks for exercise and oxygen are good; frequent interruptions are bad – because you waste time re-focusing on your subject-matter after each interruption.

Set yourself realistic (i.e. attainable) targets

If you set over-ambitious targets ('I'm going to finish this assignment tonight – even if it kills me!') and fail to achieve them, you simply reinforce your sense of guilt and failure. What you need to do is the exact opposite: set yourself targets that you can reasonably expect to achieve. Then, enjoy a sense of achievement – feel good about yourself, reward yourself in some way (a cup of tea/coffee, perhaps, or even a night off). After a break, you should feel energetic and confident enough to tackle another assignment.

Don't be too hard on yourself

Think clearly about your objectives: what precisely do you want to do? Write down your objectives, it helps you concentrate. Having clarified your objectives, and provided yourself with the necessary resources, make a start. And recognize your achievements, however modest. If you begin to punish yourself mentally (or even physically –

for example, by denying yourself that reward), you simply add to your own anxieties, reduce your performance standards and damage your chances of survival and success.

SOME PITFALLS TO EFFECTIVE STUDY

Effortless superiority is a rare phenomenon amongst students who are, after all, only human like you and me. The pursuit of excellence is quite another thing. We can all learn to derive satisfaction from exerting ourselves, mentally and physically, to the utmost of our abilities – in giving the best performance of which we're capable. Then we can allow ourselves to feel subjectively good about the outcome, whatever our objective achievement.

Try to avoid flitting from academic twig to twig. Give yourself sufficient time to get really stuck into your subject-matter. But don't drive yourself into the ground. In your first year, half an hour of concentrated thought on a specific topic may be as much as you can do at any one time. But study stints that are too short will merely increase your anxiety.

Study, as we said at the outset, may be hard work but it should also be enjoyable. Learn to share your enjoyment, as well as your problems and frustrations, with your fellow students – and your teachers, if you like. You'll spend quite long periods of time working entirely alone, but study need not be an unsociable, let alone an anti-social, process.

To survive and succeed as a student you need to discover your own personal identity and your own ways of working – but you should also discover and enjoy the comradeship of your fellow students.

SUGGESTIONS FOR FURTHER READING

Rowntree, D., *Learn How to Study* London: Macdonald, revised edition 1976, Chs. 1 and 2.

Palmer, R., and Pope, C., *Brain Train: Studying for Success* London: Spon 1984.

7 Getting the best out of lectures

*There is no more agreement about what is a good lecture
than there is about good music. Indeed, enquiries show
that different individuals require not only different
but conflicting things from a lecture. Consequently, as
most lecturers will be assessed at both extremes of a
general rating scale, any lecturer will do well if he
pleases half the audience.*
Donald Bligh: *What's the Use of Lectures* (1971)

This chapter tries to do four things:

1. To explain the purpose of lectures.
2. To suggest how to get the best out of lectures.
3. To explain how to take useful lecture notes.
4. To suggest how to make the best use of those notes.

WHY HAVE LECTURES?

In earlier centuries, scholars sat at the feet of their university teachers who expounded the Bible and other classical texts in the form of readings – or 'lectures'. A college lecture is now something quite different from a reading. Although many college teachers still have such job titles as lecturer, senior lecturer or reader, few teachers are happy reading aloud to their students for hours at a time. And students soon demonstrate their boredom. Instead, college teachers use the lecture for a variety of purposes:

1. To arouse student interest in the subject.
2. To convey information, concepts, theories about the subject.
3. To put forward their own sometimes controversial views.
4. To suggest how students may deepen their knowledge.

It's extremely doubtful whether, in these days of computer technology, information is still best conveyed by means of lectures. Yet, sad to relate, the majority of college lecturers probably still regard lectures as the primary means of getting information across to their students. Why should this be so?

1. Because the majority of college lecturers have become so familiar with lectures as the primary method of teaching, from their own student days, that they simply continue the tradition.
2. Because the majority of college lecturers probably assume (perhaps correctly) that many of their students will not acquire sufficient information, concepts and theories about the subject, except by means of lectures.
3. Because the majority of college lecturers have yet to be convinced that there are better ways of conveying information – e.g. by the use of video or computer – or are too lazy to investigate or to try them.
4. Because the majority of college lecturers are probably afraid that they might lose their students if they abandoned lectures whilst the rest of their colleagues retained them as the primary teaching method.
5. Because, deep down, the majority of college lecturers are probably frustrated actors who enjoy performing before a live audience and who, therefore, want to keep the academic lecture as a means of boosting their flagging egos.

Most college lecturers now have private doubts about the educational value of lectures. Many will be familiar with Graham

Gibbs' *Twenty Terrible Reasons for Lecturing* or Donald Bligh's *What's the Use of Lectures?* (see Suggestions for further reading at the end of this chapter) and most will have been intellectually persuaded that they ought to give fewer, better lectures and devote their remaining teaching energies to small-group learning – i.e. tutorials and seminars. Indeed, they would do so, if only they had the time or resources or if the entire teaching staff could agree to abandon lectures simultaneously. Until then, students will have to put up with some poor lectures.

HOW DO YOU GET THE BEST OUT OF LECTURES?

By being there
The first, critical point is to be there – and on time. At their first meeting with students likely to be taking their class, most teachers explain how the class will work (e.g. structure and content of syllabus, sequence of topics, suggested reading for each topic, times and place of meetings, etc.).

Lectures are often self-contained (i.e. one topic per lecture) but the benefit of lectures is cumulative. Good lecturers will often make cross references to earlier lectures. To get the most out of lectures, it pays to attend regularly. Borrowing lecture notes is often a complete waste of time because you've missed the impact.

By hearing, listening and learning
How to you stay awake in a soporific lecture? With great difficulty! But let's be generous. Let's assume our lecturers are reasonably enthusiastic about their subjects. We may still find our attention distracted by thoughts of home, family or whatever. So, we need help to focus our attention.

1. Get as close as you can (physically and mentally) to the lecturer and the lecture topic. If you sit at the back of a lecture hall, you'll get less out of it than if you sit up front.
2. Focus on the lecture topic even before the lecture begins. Go over the topic in your mind, identifying what you already know and don't know about the topic.
3. Maintain an open questioning attitude to what's being said. Train one part of your mind to listen acutely whilst another part maintains a silent, critical dialogue with the lecturer – posing questions and noting marginal comments for later follow-up (Meaning? Reasons? Evidence? Compare? etc.).

Active participation in lectures does five things:

1. It increases our attention span.
2. It helps us get at the meaning behind the lecturer's words.
3. It sharpens our critical intelligence.
4. It allows us to record the principal ideas, key concepts, competing explanatory theories and illustrations used.
5. It enables us to retain much more of the lecture content.

Don't be surprised if you retain no more than half of what is said at your first lectures. With time and practice, you'll capture much more. Competent teachers try not to convey too many ideas during first lectures but increase the 'density' of lectures over the first year.

TAKING USEFUL LECTURE NOTES

Taking notes is one of the best ways to stay alert and gain most from lectures, but how many notes and what sort? Taking lecture notes demands a different technique from taking notes from the printed page (see Chapter 8 on more effective reading and Chapter 9 on taking notes from reading). You can re-read a book – but a lecture is a unique event whose emotional impact can never be successfully reproduced, even by video-recording.

Students sometimes seek permission to record lectures: not a good idea, except perhaps in the case of some handicapped students. You don't attend a lecture to record its content verbatim. You go to be intellectually stimulated, to capture and retain its essence. The best way to do that is through the lecture notes. With practice, you can certainly capture the essential content of a lecture.

The skill of notetaking comprises six practical tasks:

1. *Concentrate on essentials* Go for the main points of the lecture, not details. Lecturers often give an overview at the start of a lecture and a summary at the end. Watch out for these. Take as few notes as possible but sufficient to enable you to recall and revise all the essential content – that is, the key ideas, concepts, theories, etc.
2. *Try to capture the architectural shape of the lecture* Think of your notes as a skeleton or outline of the lecture you'll give to your fellow students who are absent. Bring out the overall design, shape and sequence of the arguments deployed by the lecturer.
3. *Use bold capitals, headlines, sub-heads and underlining* Provide

plenty of guideposts and signs to assist later retrieval and revision. Distinguish major from minor points and provide plenty of light and shade.

4. *Jot down words and phrases, not whole sentences* You haven't time to record exactly what's said (except for exact titles of books, etc.), so keep notes brief. You can fill out your outline when you revise your notes for essays or exams. Keep your notes clear and uncluttered. Don't begrudge the cost of the paper!

5. *Use diagrams wherever possible* You don't need to be a graphic artist. Use blocks and circles to link trains of thought and to feature significant connections and relationships. Use colour if you think it helps.

6. *Keep your notes legible* Notes must be in a form in which they can serve you later. Illegible notes are more trouble than they are worth. You'll get little or no value from notes taken on scrappy paper, which can't be filed and retrieved at will or which are difficult to decipher. You can train yourself to write faster and legibly. Practise it!

The acid test is this: will you be able to read through your notes the next day and recapture the essential arguments used by the lecturer? You'll never be asked to reproduce the whole of a lecture. You may be asked to discuss intelligently the essential subject-matter of a lecture.

Too many notes simply obscure the overall shape and conceal the essential content of a lecture. So, go for skeleton notes – and leave plenty of margins and space round your notes. Don't begrudge the paper! You'll find you'll need that space to write marginal notes (e.g. to make connections), to add queries and follow-up points when you come to re-read your notes for revision purposes (see Chapter 13 on pass those exams – and stay human).

HOW TO MAKE THE BEST USE OF LECTURE NOTES

Research evidence shows that, just as student attention fades significantly during the course of a lecture, so the retention and recall of lecture material fades equally rapidly. How can you make the best use of lecture notes?

1. *Read your notes within twenty-four hours* By reading your notes, you reinforce learning and prevent too-rapid fading of lecture material. Fill gaps, identify queries and note points for immediate follow up. Remember to take up these queries in tutorials/seminars.

2. *File your notes at least weekly* Even your best lecture notes are useless if you can't find them. Develop an index of notes that really helps you locate notes quickly when preparing for tutorials, writing essays or revising for exams. A simple, box filing-system is invaluable.
3. *Edit your notes every term* Editing means re-reading, amending, cross-referencing and improving your notes by enriching their content. Underline, use colour-coding for highlighting – do anything that makes your notes more lively, vivid and memorable.

SUGGESTIONS FOR FURTHER READING

Gibbs, G., *Teaching Students to Learn*, Milton Keynes: OU Press, 1981
Bligh, D., *What's the use of Lectures?* Dundee: A & B Bligh, 2nd edn. revised, 1972.

8 More effective reading

*We asked anyone who could do so to write a short
statement about what the chapter was about. The
number who were able to tell us . . . was just one in a
hundred-fifteen. As a demonstration of
purposelessness in the reading of 99% of freshmen,
we found this impressive . . . When we pointed the
ending out to them, some said 'You mean you can
sometimes tell what a chapter is about by looking at the
end' and others said 'O Lord, how many times have I
been told!'*

    William Perry, 'Students' Use and Misuse of Reading
    Skills', *Harvard Educational Review* (1959)

This chapter tries to do three things:

1. To help you find out where to start reading.
2. To help you understand about different kinds of reading.
3. To help you improve your reading skills.

WHERE TO START READING?

Most students say they enjoy reading. Few have thought carefully about what 'reading for a college degree or diploma' involves. Reading for pleasure and reading for profitable study are not the same. To survive and succeed at college, you must learn (1) what to read (2) how to read, and (3) how to take useful notes and then to make the best use of them (see Chapter 9 on taking notes from reading).

On first entering your college library, you may well feel daunted by the sight of so many books and journals. Where do you begin? Do not despair! There is help at hand.

1. Find out if the library runs a slide-tape presentation. You should learn the lay-out of the library and discover how to use the catalogues, bibliographies, microfiches, on-line computer terminals and reference sections. Most of these will carry instructions that are 'user-friendly'. But if you run into problems, make friends with the helpful staff at the enquiry desks.
2. Don't be put off by the bewildering choice of reading. You will be guided by your class teachers on what to read and where to begin. Make sure you get a copy of the initial (and any supplementary) reading list(s) handed out at the first meeting with your class teachers.
3. Buy the latest (preferably paperback) edition of the main recommended textbook for each course/class. If you are in doubt about which textbook to buy, consult your class teacher – and watch the departmental notice boards for offers of second-hand books.
4. Become familiar with the academic conventions for citing books and other readings, e.g.:

> Friedman, Henry, and Meredeen, Sander, *The Dynamics of Industrial Conflict: Lessons from Ford*, London: Croom Helm, 1980.

> Lockyer, C.J., 'How Tomorrow's Workforce Sees Management and Unions', *Personnel Management*, Vol. 14, No. 8, August 1982, pp. 42–4.

5. Don't be afraid to ask for reading priorities. Your class teacher may recommend specific chapters, extracts or articles for particular tutorial topics. But don't expect to find the answers to all your questions in any one single text. Learn to be eclectic – i.e. selective – but fairly singleminded in your pursuit of answers.
6. Don't become frustrated if the particular book or journal you

want is not on the shelf where you'd expect to find it, just when you want it. If you plan your reading well ahead of your tutorials or essay-writing deadline, you stand a better chance of getting hold of the books you want. A book not in its correct place on the library shelf may be:

(a)   in use in the library;
(b)   out on loan to another borrower;
(c)   misplaced on the shelves; or
(d)   missing and not yet replaced.

Self-help in these circumstances is an unqualified virtue, but do ask the library staff to help if you've repeatedly failed to find the text you're looking for. Persevere in tracking down the text you want. Make use of your municipal branch library; your inter-county library loan service; the departmental library, etc. As a final resort, ask your class teachers whether they have a spare copy to lend you. They can only say 'no'. If you borrow a book make sure you return it as soon as possible.

DIFFERENT KINDS OF READING

Contrary to popular belief, not all students know how to read when they first arrive at college. Functional literacy (the ability to read) is one thing; learning how to get the most out of your college reading is quite another. Yet the ability to read with attention, to increase your reading speed, to improve your comprehension, to assess critically the strengths of competing arguments and to take useful notes – these are all vitally important study skills.

In his book, *Learn how to Study* (see Suggestions for further reading at the end of this chapter), Derek Rowntree offers excellent advice on how to tackle a textbook. He quotes the words of Francis Bacon in the sixteenth century: 'Some books are to be tasted, others to be swallowed and some few to be chewed and digested.' Rowntree adapts Bacon's advice in this way:

1.   *Tasting* – i.e. referring to isolated passages in the text.
2.   *Swallowing* – i.e. skimming lightly and rapidly through the whole text.
3.   *Chewing and digesting* – i.e. studying the whole of a text carefully with close attention.

HOW TO IMPROVE YOUR READING SKILLS

Having chosen a text, you must decide which method best suits your purpose. The method recommended by Rowntree is *S Q 3R* – the initial letters of the first steps to better reading. Used flexibly and intelligently, *S Q 3R* is an invaluable guide:

S – survey: tackle the whole before you tackle the detailed parts
Surveying gives you the measure of the task before you. Survey the book first, then the chapter, then the paragraph. Pay special attention to:

1. title page for edition and year of publication;
2. contents page for book's overall structure;
3. index for key entries and emphases;
4. chapter headings as signposts to detailed contents;
5. first and last chapters for aims and conclusions;
6. first and last paragraphs of each chapter for summaries;
7. section sub-headings for signposts on detailed arguments; and
8. first and last sentences of paragraphs for detailed arguments.

Q – question: never read without first having some questions in mind
Questioning helps to keep your mind fresh and alert. Think what you already know and what you now want to know. Ask yourself:

1. What does this author set out to do?
2. What does he or she say that's new and interesting?
3. What does he or she mean by what he or she says?
4. Does what he or she says support/supplement/contradict what I already know or believe?

1R – read: never read passively but critically with full attention.
Don't expect to understand everything at a first reading. At a first reading:

1. look for the main (and secondary) ideas;
2. get the general shape and subject-matter clear; and
3. don't attempt to take notes – or mark the page!

At a second reading:

1. follow the detailed reasoning or argument;

2.   note what you missed at the first reading;
3.   if you own the book, you may mark key points; and
4.   if you don't own the book, note key points. (See Chapter 9 on taking notes from reading.)

2R – recall: check your understanding of what you've read
Recall helps to sustain concentration when you read. It helps to correct misunderstandings. It keeps your reading active rather than passive. Ask yourself:

1.   How much do I remember?
2.   How well did I understand?
3.   How much can I explain in my own words?
4.   Can I recall key points without re-reading the text?

3R – review: a further viewing of the text to check your recall
Review tells you how much you've really taken in. Repeat the previous four steps – i.e.:

1.   Survey – check headings and summaries.
2.   Question – do new questions arise?
3.   Re-read – have you missed anything important?
4.   Recall – fill gaps and correct faults in notes.

FASTER READING WITH BETTER COMPREHENSION

If you consistently practise the ideas offered in this chapter, you should get a lot more out of your reading. You should read much faster with greater comprehension and greater retention. Try these exercises to improve your reading skills:

1.   Pass your eyes faster over the page of print.
2.   *Don't* sub-vocalize the text – you'll still understand more.
3.   Time a standard page of text and practise faster reading.
4.   Avoid eye-strain and have your sight checked regularly.

SUGGESTIONS FOR FURTHER READING

Buzan, T., *Use Your Head!*, London: BBC Publications, 1974.
Rowntree, D., *Learn how to Study*, London: Macdonald Paperback, revised edition, 1976.

9 Taking effective notes from reading

Students in the having mode of existence will . . . write down every word in their looseleaf notebook – so that, later on, they can memorise their notes and thus pass an examination. But the content does not become part of their own individual system of thought, enriching and widening it . . . Instead . . . each student has become the owner of a collection of statements made by somebody else (who had either created them or taken them over from another source).

Erich Fromm, *To Have or To Be?* (1976)

This chapter tries to do three things:

1. To explain the importance of taking effective notes.
2. To help you to take more effective notes.
3. To suggest how to make the best use of your notes.

WHY TAKE NOTES?

According to B.F. Skinner, 'Education is what survives when what has been taught has been forgotten' ('Education in 1984', see Suggestions for further reading at the end of this chapter). He was evidently not facing the college class and exams that you're facing! A cynic might define education as the notes that survive after you pass (or fail) your exams. Whichever view you take, good notes will help you to enjoy and to get the most out of your studies and to achieve a better degree result.

Note-taking encourages active learning and provides you with some written record of what you've been studying. But notes must be well taken. The backs of old envelopes may be good enough for shopping lists but scrappy notes are worse than none. They simply increase your panic when you most need help. Notes should therefore be taken in a consistent format that allows you the greatest flexibility when it comes to using them. For example, a loose-leaf binder is better than an exercise book because you can shuffle and re-classify your notes for tutorials, essay-writing and later exam revision.

Students are often uncertain whether they are taking the right kind of notes to help them survive and succeed at college. Here are some practical guidenotes to help you master this critical study skill.

HOW TO TAKE MORE EFFECTIVE NOTES

How much note-taking?
The aim should be to take brief, intelligible notes that will assist your recall of key points within the structure and sequence of the argument. Most students take far too many notes. You need as few words and symbols on your page as possible. However, note-taking is a highly individual matter. You must devise your own style, format, abbreviations, etc., for yourself.

What to note?
You need to capture the main ideas and the line of argument. Go for the key points – the points that sustain the argument and help to clinch it. The advice offered in Chapter 8 on more effective reading was that you should only begin to take notes after a first reading – when you've grasped the structure and got the gist of the topic being dealt with.

The same general advice holds good: concentrate on following the flow of the argument and jot down just the key points within a coherent structure. Ideal notes take on the character of architecture – that is, they comprise a well-defined structure; they are capable of supporting and containing the burden to be later placed on them; and they are designed to last. If your notes are well structured, you can nearly always fill in the decorative details later.

How best to structure your notes?

Europeans tend to structure their notes (and their thinking) in linear fashion – that is, from top to bottom and from left to right on the page. There's nothing wrong with that, provided you leave sufficient margins to the left (for file bindings) and to the right (for later commentaries). Good reading notes taken by a good student will approximate to the structure of the author's chapter, book or article – they will include all key points but will omit the more detailed points.

In his fascinating book, *Use Your Head!* Tony Buzan recommends an exciting alternative approach to note-taking. He argues that our brains do not work in straight lines. So, instead of linear notes, he urges us to adopt the 'starburst' approach to note-taking. Buzan claims that this pattern of note-taking conforms more closely to the pattern of our thinking and is, therefore, more useful for later recall, for preparing tutorial questions or revising a topic for an exam. This method may be more suitable for some subjects than for others – try it and see if it meets your needs.

Compare the examples of linear and starburst note-taking from lectures in Figures 9.1 and 9.2. (The same two methods may be used to take notes from reading.) If you've been used to linear note-taking for many years, you'll need to persevere with the Buzan method.

LECTURE 1: INTRO TO ECONOMICS
1   Markets and market forces
            Private sector
            Entrepreneurs
            State encouragement/discouragement
2   Supply & demand
            Disposable income
            Affordable prices (marginal utility theory)
            Luxury goods vs necessities
            Fashion goods
            Reliability of goods/sces
3   Factors of prodn
            Land – rent of
            Labour – wages and salaries; fringe benefits; taxes
            Capital – rate of interest
            Cost of factors vary through time
4   Scale of prodn
            Craft workshops (e.g. carpenter)
            Mass prodn (e.g. car assembly lines)
            Hi-tech (e.g. oil refineries)
            Costs/profits
5   Competition
            Home vs overseas markets
            Perfect vs imperfect competition

Figure 9.1   Example of linear notes

ECONOMICS (1)

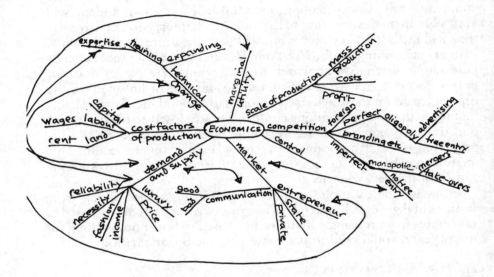

Figure 9.2   Example of starburst notes.
Buzan suggests first taking 'linear' notes from lectures and converting them to 'starburst' notes for revision.

HOW TO MAKE THE BEST USE OF YOUR NOTES

Re-reading your notes

Having taken notes (in whichever format), you must learn how best to use them. It's pointless to take notes and then put them away until exam revision. You should first re-read your notes within twenty-four hours of having taken them. That first re-reading reinforces the learning process and helps to fix the essential points in your memory. As you re-read your notes, you should add further marginal comments to those taken during the lecture/tutorial (Meaning? Evidence? Compare/contrast, follow up, etc.).

Editing your notes
You should edit your notes, just as you might edit a computer file. You need to make connections between notes taken from your recent reading and notes taken earlier. Cross-reference the main ideas. Compare and contrast different theories, viewpoints and illustrations. In this way, you enrich your learning.

Filing your notes
You then need to devise a filing and retrieval system that allows you to find the notes on a given topic when you want them. Try using any substantial cardboard box as a simple but effective filing cabinet. Set up a simple card-index system to log your notes in and out. Some students find it best to set aside a regular time each week (perhaps at the weekend) to file all the notes taken during the previous week.

Classifying your notes
You can classify and index your notes for later use by subject, author or likely use. Most important, you can build up a collection of notes as part of your own library of books, newspaper cuttings, essays and other materials that you should find invaluable for tutorials, essays, projects and exam revision.

Don't throw anything away at this stage
There will come a time when you need to go through your notes and weed out what's no longer required. But beware of over-hasty discarding of notes. Keep your notes for at least a full year – and probably for the whole length of the course. You'll be surprised how often you need to refer back to earlier work. In this way, nothing is wasted.

SUGGESTIONS FOR FURTHER READING

Buzan, T., *Use Your Head!*, London: BBC Publications, 1974.
Fromm, E., *To Have or To Be?*, London: Abacus, 1974.

10 Getting the most out of tutorials / seminars

The (tutorial) system therefore counters perhaps the greatest enemy of intellectual progress amongst undergraduates: the passive collection of unanalysed material. Far from being . . . a system that makes things easy . . . it is one that demands the greatest effort and initiative . . . but in such a way that is within reach of all.

J.P. Corbett, in *The Idea of a New University* (ed.)
David Daiches (1964)

This chapter tries to do three things:

1. To explain what purpose a tutorial / seminar serves.
2. To recommend how best to prepare for tutorials.
3. To help you get the most out of your tutorials.

WHY HAVE TUTORIALS?

A lecture course is often a passive form of learning: you listen acutely and take notes but are generally discouraged from asking questions or raising points because the size of the group inhibits fruitful exchanges.

By contrast, a tutorial group (or seminar) should be small enough to allow all its members to participate fully in the discussion.

At Oxford and some other colleges, a 'Tutorial' is the name for weekly/fortnightly meeting with your tutor (sometimes shared with one or two other students) to read and discuss your written assignment. Elsewhere a 'tutorial' is simply the name for a small learning group. Whatever its name, the tutorial or small learning group provides a uniquely-valuable opportunity to increase your understanding of any subject and to develop your skill in exchanging intellectual ideas. So you should certainly learn to make the most of it.

The most important point to understand is that a tutorial is an opportunity to share in the learning process: to share your ideas, experience, understanding and perplexities. That means there's no such thing as a 'silly' question in a tutorial – provided it's relevant. And there's no opting out: the price of admission to a tutorial is that every student shares in the discussion. As the Americans say, 'There's no free lunch!'

HOW TO PREPARE FOR TUTORIALS

In most tutorial groups, in Arts, Social Science and Business, students take it in turn to open the discussion. Whether you've been asked to open the discussion or not, you should prepare yourself for the tutorial as follows:

1. *Think carefully about the meaning of the question(s)* Questions may be straightforward or they may be deliberately provocative. Try to identify the heart of the matter the question is getting at. Concentrate on that question and begin by asking yourself how much you already know about the question.
2. *Revise your lecture notes, if any, on the topic* Try to relate the topic under discussion to what you've heard in lectures. Use your lecture notes to help you identify what's essential and what's marginal to the question posed.
3. *Read and note as many of the recommended texts as possible* Your tutor will guide you on what to read. Try to gather a diversity of views, not just one approach to the question. It's the clash or conflict of views that helps to illuminate the question.
4. *Identify what you know/understand – and what you don't* Remember, there's no shame in admitting that you don't understand something you've read. You could find yourself in greater difficulties later if you don't grasp basic concepts and ideas in the early stages of the class. Don't be afraid to ask for help.
5. *List the key points you wish to raise for discussion* To get help

with what you don't understand, list the points you want to raise in discussion. Make sure you raise those points early in the tutorial. Don't wait until the last few minutes; it may be too late. Don't assume another student will ask your question.

6.   *Try to relate this topic to earlier/later topics* Tutorial topics rarely exist in a vacuum. There is often a cluster of topics around a subject or theme. Try to make relevant connections between different topics, both within and between your class subjects.

In Science, Engineering and Technology, tutorials are likely to be devoted to problem–solving. You are usually given problems in advance, and will be asked to give your solutions and how you arrived at them.

HOW TO GET THE MOST OUT OF YOUR TUTORIALS

If you are asked to open the discussion

Most students feel nervous before opening any discussion. It's the same for your fellow students. And you get better with practice. Here are some suggestions to help.

1.   Summarize your essential points on one page. Just the essential points – not an essay!
2.   Say how you intend to approach/tackle the question.
3.   Provide some definition or clarification of your subject-matter.
4.   Utilize relevant concepts, alternative theories and perspectives.
5.   Present key facts, opinions, views, with source references.
6.   Tell us what you think. Don't just recite what 'Bloggs' says.

Note: Use black print on white paper to facilitate reproduction. If possible, duplicate and distribute copies well in advance of the tutorial. Don't begrudge the cost. You'll acquire valuable revision notes. Don't forget to include your tutor!

How to open the discussion

1.   Check that all members of the group have read your summary.
2.   Make a brief effective verbal presentation of your case.
3.   Concentrate on what you find interesting, provoking, perplexing.
4.   Say what you don't understand and ask the group for help.
5.   Pose questions you would like the group to discuss.
6.   Don't tell us all you know on the topic – that's boring!
7.   Don't read your paper – learn to improvize from notes or headings.
8.   Open up the topic for discussion – don't close it down!
9.   Don't exceed about ten minutes. You'll be stopped after fifteen.

If you are not opening the discussion
This doesn't mean you can relax – not if you want to get the most out of your tutorials. Your tutor may still call on you to give your own views. Here's how you might prepare for these tutorials:

1. Make sure you obtain and read the summary well in advance.
2. Note the key points and questions you wish to raise for discussion.
3. During the presentation, listen carefully and take brief notes.
4. After the presentation, ask questions and express views.

Note: This does *not* mean monopolizing the tutorial with long speeches. It *does* mean learning to cultivate the exchange of ideas and viewpoints.

Don't allow your attention to drift. Stick with the discussion and offer your contribution to the group. You'll get much more out of the tutorial and feel you 'belong', once you've become a regular contributing member of the learning group.

Rationale for the advice offered here
You only get out of a tutorial what you are prepared to put into it – plus a little bit more! Your tutor is there as a resource and will keep things moving. But it's up to you to play the major roles. Remember, you may never get the same chance to try out your ideas – however half-baked – and still be treated kindly by your fellow students. If you have an idea, let's hear it. It may be brilliant – so it would be selfish not to share it with others. If you don't understand something, say so – you'll be surprised how many others don't understand either! Learn to overcome your shyness: it will stand you in good stead for the rest of your life. Learn how to disagree with the arguments put forward by others without making them feel small. Try to bring in relevant points from other courses and sources, including your personal experience.
The rationale for all this is:

1. it prevents the group from becoming bored and frustrated;
2. it trains you to identify essentials and to avoid waffle;
3. it gives you practice in handling intellectual exchanges;
4. it increases your sensitivity to the feelings of others;
5. it helps you to 'think on your feet' and gain self-confidence;
6. it assists you with later revision and exam techniques; and
7. it makes for better learning and it's more fun.

Having the last word
Whether or not you opened the discussion, you may be invited to have the last word. Be ready to say what you believe you've learned from the

discussion. Remember, a tutorial offers an opportunity for sociable learning: so learn to make the most of your tutorials by your participation. Participation makes for better learning and makes that learning more enjoyable.

SUGGESTIONS FOR FURTHER READING

Gibbs, G., *Learning to Study* Cambridge: National Extension College, 1981.
Main, A., *Encouraging Effective Learning*, Edinburgh: Scottish Academic Press, 1980.

11 Better college writing*

Some students think that all good writers come to their task in a well-organized frame of mind – outline intact, computer ready. Would that this were true. Most writers go through a series of fumbling stages, groping for ideas, before they manage to sort them out and develop an organized plan. Eventually they must develop that plan, of course, but the pathway is criss-crossed with distracting side trails that can lead the writer astray.

Cavender and Weiss, *Thinking/Writing* (1987)

This chapter tries to do three things:

1. To help you understand what's meant by better college writing.
2. To help you write your first essays.
3. To help you improve your writing skills.

* This chapter was written with the help of Professor John Midgeley and Dr Carolyn Converse, Department of Pharmacy, University of Strathclyde.

WHAT IS COLLEGE WRITING?

Writing forms an essential part of college work. Most students enjoy reading, but dislike having to write. Perhaps they've never been taught to write or how to handle criticism of their written work. Whatever the reasons may be, the ability to express your own ideas clearly, logically and concisely is an important study skill to be developed.

Written work at college is generally of two kinds: (1) essays, reports or other written assignments; (2) examination answers. In both areas, you need to learn how to communicate your ideas as effectively as possible through the written word – whether in handwritten, typed or word-processed form (see Chapter 13 on Pass those exams).

An essay in Arts, Social Science and Business is an intellectual exercise and an aesthetic challenge: you attempt to structure your thoughts and to express your own ideas on a particular topic or question in a concise, elegant and persuasive written form. An essay tests your ability to analyse a given question, to develop a line of argument, to explain clearly what you mean and to express a point of view so as to persuade – if not always to convince – the reader of the strength of your case. To be persuasive your meaning needs to be clear. An essay in Science, Engineering or Technology may call for a survey of the literature on a specific topic. It should provide a readable condensation of the recent literature: a critical appraisal, not a mere catalogue.

A report is similar to an essay but often contains an account of a discussion, the summary findings of a piece of research or of the literature on a given theme.

Drafting a Scientific Paper requires a more closely-prescribed format:

1.   Abstract – a concise summary
2.   Introduction – which places the work in a historial context and explains why it was thought important and worthwhile.
3.   Materials and Methods – which describes the experiment or procedures undertaken.
4.   Results – which states the experimental results obtained and provides illustrative examples.
5.   Discussion – which develops conclusions and incorporates them into the historical pattern of evolving knowledge, perhaps offering some conjectures but avoiding speculation.

WRITING YOUR FIRST ESSAYS

Careful preparation and consistently self-critical writing pay dividends. Before you begin to write, prepare yourself as follows:

1. *Think carefully about the meaning of the question/subject posed* The same question may admit to several different interpretations. Move from the abstract to the concrete in your thinking. Break large tasks down into smaller, more manageable parts. You might begin by writing notes and questions to yourself – to check what you already know and where you need more information.

2. *Muster your resources* You're unlikely to be stimulated by a blank sheet of paper. You must learn to interact with your notes and other resources. Don't lose sight of the time and space constraints. Don't put off your writing until the last minute and then panic.

3. *Decide on an approach – how you intend to tackle the question* Will you adopt the obvious approach or take an unorthodox line? Experiment by all means – but keep a sense of proportion.

4. *Develop an appropriate structure/outline of your essay* You may develop alternative structures and then combine them. Check that your structure will give shape and coherence to your essay. A good structure is one which:

   (a) ensures that you cover all essential points;
   (b) provides a solid foundation on which to build your argument;
   (c) holds your argument together without undue strain;
   (d) offers sufficient scope to develop your argument; and
   (e) enables you to reach your conclusion.

One suggested essay structure might be as follows;

1. *Introduction* – in which you say how you interpret the question and how you intend to tackle it. You should establish your line of argument right at the outset.

2. *Section 1* – in which you present your principal arguments in clearly differentiated paragraphs.

3. *Section 2, 3, etc.* – in which you develop your argument, offer supporting or qualifying evidence, cite relevant authorities and otherwise make your case convincing.

4. *Conclusion* – in which you clinch the argument by threading together your earlier points, making your overall position unambiguously clear without tedious repetition. A good conclusion emerges; it needs no super-glue.

The writing task

Here are some pointers on how to go about the writing task:

1.   Write a first draft of your essay. Don't get 'hung up' on your first sentence or paragraph; they're always the most difficult. Keep writing – and come back to them later.
2.   Put your draft aside for a couple of days. Stop worrying about the essay and turn to something completely different.
3.   Re-read your draft with a sharply-critical eye – as if you were a constructive critic of another student's work. Ask yourself (a) whether the writer tells you what he or she is trying to do; (b) whether they succeed in doing it; and (c) whether they convince you it was worth doing!
4.   Pay close attention to the opening sentence of your first paragraph and the closing sentence of your last paragraph. They continue to reverberate in your reader's mind.
5.   Identify and correct weaknesses of presentation, argument, expression, style and spelling. Reduce for overlength.
6.   Make sure you've remembered to list your references and to provide a list of sources consulted. Respect the academic conventions when citing authors and titles.
7.   Check that your own name, the name of your tutor, the title of the essay and the course are displayed clearly and prominently at the top of page one.
8.   Make a clear, legible copy of your final version – leaving sufficient space for your tutor to add marginal comments.
9.   Retain a spare copy for your file. The original may be lost.
10.   Make sure the essay is handed in on time.

HOW TO IMPROVE YOUR WRITING SKILLS

Pay close attention to your tutor's critical but constructive comments on all your essays. With practice, you will gradually develop your own critical faculties and become more self-critical. Until then, here are some further hints on how to improve your essay-writing:

1.   Make sure your essay has answered the question. Check that promises made in good faith in your first paragraph have been delivered by your last paragraph.
2.   Check your essay for relevance. Your tutor may be generous to a fault but cannot reward irrelevance or peripheral knowledge display.
3.   Conciseness is a virtue – so express yourself economically. Avoid waffle or padding. A good essay, like a good kilt / skirt, is long enough to be decent but short enough to be interesting.
4.   Don't assume that the reader already understands your argument or automatically shares your viewpoint. To be persuasive, you need to clarify your position, make your assumptions explicit and your meaning as clear as possible.

5. Don't waste precious time stating the obvious. By being subtle rather than obvious, you avoid appearing naïve. Take an unconventional line, by all means, but avoid mere displays of cleverness. Unless they are quite brilliant, jokes are best avoided in essays. Avoid clichés like the plague!

6. Use relevant scientific and technical concepts to help build your case. Personal reminiscences and anecdotes have no place in an academic essay. Avoid making unsubstantiated assertions. Provide evidence for your arguments throughout.

7. Use language appropriate to your context and subject-matter. Avoid slang, jargon and colloquial expressions that might be perfectly acceptable in speech but that are out of place in an academic essay. Vulgarisms may make good graffiti but they are not appropriate in an academic essay.

8. Make connections that help your writing to flow more easily and allow your meaning to emerge more clearly. Learn to use linking devices that help to bind your argument together more tightly.

9. Don't 'anthologize'. An essay is not simply an anthology of other people's ideas. The reader wants to know what *you* think – so avoid excessive or extensive quotations from others.

10. Correct punctuation is neither an irrelevant luxury nor a pedantic affectation: it conveys and alters exact meaning. Learn how to use the apostrophe (to indicate either possession or contraction, not plurals!), especially in association with the three consecutive letters *i, t* and *s*. Master its correct usage today and it's no problem tomorrow.

11. Take pride in your writer's craft. Don't be ashamed of having to re-write a sentence or paragraph several times to make your meaning still clearer. Refer to a dictionary or a thesaurus of synonyms, antonyms, etc., when you're uncertain about the precise meaning or spelling of an unusual word.

12. Finally, avoid sexist language – but don't go overboard. 'Skilled workers' refers to both men and women but 'manpower' is still manpower. The rights of man remain inviolate, like mankind or Manchester. But learn to use 'he or she' or, more elegantly, 'they, them or theirs', as appropriate rather than the male form of the pronoun all the time.

SUGGESTIONS FOR FURTHER READING

Cavender, N. and Weiss, L., *Thinking/Writing*, Belmont, CA.: Wadsworth, 1987.

Gowers, E., *The Complete Plain Words*, Harmondsworth: Penguin, 1962.

12 Critical thinking and problem-solving

*Bertrand Russell complained that he spent his first year
at Cambridge looking in vain for the cleverest young
men in the world who, he had been assured, were there.
In his second year it dawned on him that he and his
friends were the cleverest young men in the world.*
Matthew Parris, *The Sunday Times* review of *The
Oxford Myth*, edited by Rachel Johnston (June 1988)

This chapter tries to do three things:

1. To explain why students need critical thinking skills.
2. To discover whether you already know how to think.
3. To show how to apply critical thinking to your studies.

WHY DO WE NEED TO THINK CRITICALLY?

Although we may now know much more about the chemistry of the
human brain, our capacity for thought has probably not changed
much over the past five thousand years. 'I think', said Descartes,

'therefore I am'. But how do I think? What am I capable of thinking? And how can that thinking help solve my own and the world's problems?

Critical and creative thinking are now fashionable on American campuses and amongst intellectuals generally – perhaps because many thinking Americans believe the 'Great Society' has failed to solve sufficient of its most urgently-critical domestic problems – like drugs, violence, corruption, homelessness and the budget deficit – quite apart from its most pressing international problems – like relations with the Soviet Union, the mid-East and Latin-American crises, and so on.

Critical and creative thinking may be just another buzz phrase for thinking. But the different ways in which thought can be creatively applied to both mental and practical problems are indispensable tools for student success. When Marx wanted to highlight the philosophical contradictions underlying bourgeois social morality, he inverted the usual formulation – the philosophy of poverty – and wrote instead about the poverty of philosophy.

Problems, puzzles and policy issues

Puzzles are mental tasks or games that present some intellectual challenge but are easily solved. For example, how do I get a quart of soup into a pint pot? Flippant answer: Drink half the soup! Serious answer: Condense the soup by boiling off half its water content.

Policy issues concern high-level strategy questions, whose character and complexity involve the examination of vast quantities of data before decisions can be taken on matters of the highest political import. For example, what should the government's policy be towards First Secretary Gorbachov's attempt at *perestroika* (economic and social reconstruction within the Soviet Union)? Answer: many policy issues admit to no immediately-obvious solution. The issues are probably too complex to be adequately dealt with here, but the government should certainly give Gorbachov's initiative every encouragement because it seems to be in this country's own long-term interests.

Problems lie somewhere between puzzles and policy issues. A problem might be defined, somewhat abstractly perhaps, as an unsolved mental or physical task that derives from an observed deviation from the standard or norm expected. Problems may vary considerably in their complexity but are almost invariably susceptible to solution, given time and sufficient critical and creative thought. For example, how to land allied armies and vast quantities of supplies on the beaches of enemy-occupied Normandy during the Second World War? Answer: Mulberry Harbour – a pre-fabricated, sectional, floating harbour, designed and built in Britain and successfully assembled on the beaches of Arromanches.

SO, YOU ALREADY KNOW HOW TO THINK?

At school, you are rewarded for knowing the right answers. You dare not be wrong. When schoolteachers ask questions, they already know the answers and are simply checking to make sure you know them, too. At college, the questions you and your fellow students pose are as important as the answers supplied. Your answers are likely to be just as right or wrong as those of your teachers. In fact, college teachers are probably more interested in the reasoning by which you reach your answer than they are in the substantive answer itself. In other words, they are concerned with the process of intellectual enquiry – with teaching you to learn how to think for yourself.

You may think you're quite good at solving mental problems. If so, try this one for size:

Critical thinking problem 12.1 (See the end of this chapter for answer.) I have three boxes. Inside each of these boxes, I have two smaller boxes. And, inside each of these smaller boxes, I have three yet smaller boxes. How many boxes do I have altogether?

Dr Julia Thomason, a leading exponent of critical and creative thinking at Appalachian State University, North Carolina, says students are likely to react to this type of problem in one of four different ways:

1. There are evasive strategists – those who say: 'I don't do that type of problem!'
2. There are concrete operational thinkers – those who can only begin to solve such a problem in concrete operational terms by drawing physical or mental images of the boxes and then counting up the total.
3. There are transitional thinkers – those who soon make the conceptual transition from the concrete to the more abstract form of the problem – one that is capable of being solved by a combination of multiplication and addition.
4. There are formal operational thinkers – those who immediately grasp the abstract form of the problem and solve it quickly and easily.

This problem illustrates the simple point that there is no one way of thinking. Different individuals, at different times, think about problems in different ways. They use alternative, but equally valid, methods of thinking to arrive at their answers. Since not all problems are the same, some call for one type of thinking rather than another.

Critical thinking problem 12.2 (See the end of this chapter for answer.) Descend into a mysterious world, using the same three letters twice, in exactly the same order:

– – – E R G R O – – –

This is essentially a linguistic problem, whose solution probably depends as much upon the range of your vocabulary, and your response to the stimulus of words, rather than upon your capacity to reason formally through a set of data in order to arrive at a valid solution.

Critical thinking problem 12.3 (See end of this chapter for answer.) Complete the following seven-word description of Ferdinand de Lesseps (the man behind the building of the Panama Canal) in such a way that the solution is palindromic, i.e. it is capable of being read both backwards and forewords:

A – A –, A – – A –, A – A – A –: – A – A – A

Here again, whilst formal logic will not necessarily solve the problem, there are several clues contained within the problem itself.

Critical thinking problem 12.4 (See end of this chapter for answer.) There is a terrible car crash. The driver and passenger – the driver's child – are rushed to hospital where the senior surgeon is called upon to operate immediately to save the child's life. Although the child is still alive, at the last minute the surgeon refuses to operate. Can you suggest why?

The problem here is more open-ended. There could be many possible reasons why the surgeon refuses to operate. Try processing all the relevant information contained in the problem to help you come up with one plausible explanation.

Critical thinking problem 12.5 (See end of this chapter for answer.) An unusually warm day in May, with temperatures soaring and a very high pollen count. The library crowded with students, frantically revising for imminent exams. Student A, overcome by the heat, flings open a window. Student B immediately slams it shut, complaining bitterly of hay fever. A quarrel ensues, distracting every student within earshot. Two factions emerge: the 'closed' and the 'open' window brigades. The librarian, called to deal with the situation, finds no apparent room for compromise: a window must be either open or shut. How might she still resolve the dispute by creative thinking?

If these examples reveal anything, perhaps it is the unwelcome truth that most of us are better at memorizing and applying formulae for solving certain types of predictable problems than we are at generating imaginative solutions to unfamiliar problems. Yet the world we live in cries out for more critical and creative solutions to many, pressing problems. One example is the Camp David Accords, worked out between Egypt and the State of Israel, with the help of President Carter and his officials and signed in 1979.

In essence the problem was this: Israel refused to withdraw its armed forces from the area of Sinai, captured after Arab armies invaded its territory during the 1973 Yom Kippur War, unless and until Egypt would guarantee the integrity of their new common frontier. Egypt was one of several Arab states that had attacked Israel and that hitherto had refused to formally recognize the state's existence, let alone guarantee its frontiers. It now refused to budge from that position unless and until Israel withdrew its armed forces from occupied Sinai. This seemingly irreconcilable impasse was resolved by President Carter and his staff who encouraged both sides to take the risk of thinking more critically and creatively about solving their joint problems, along the following lines.

For a variety of diplomatic and other reasons, Egypt wanted Sinai (largely desert) back in Egyptian hands. Israel did not want Sinai as such but insisted on the military security of its southern borders. Israel refused to give up Sinai without some significant concession on Egypt's part. Israel was eventually persuaded to withdraw its tanks to new, secure positions, well back from the Sinai, thus allowing Egypt to achieve some part of its principal aims – on condition that Egypt, for its part, formally recognized the State of Israel and respected the new border, thus allowing Israel to secure some part of its own principal aims. Despite the assassination of one of the leading co-signatories, Egyptian President Sadat, and the death of the other, Israeli Prime Minister Begin, the Camp David Accords have been respected by both sides ever since their signing in 1979.

HOW TO APPLY CRITICAL THINKING TO YOUR STUDY PROBLEMS

Students frequently say they have done the recommended reading, taken the necessary notes and reviewed all their materials, but still cannot come up with a solution to the problem posed. Where, they ask, do you find the ideas to solve such a problem?

Ideas do not exist in a vacuum, free-floating in outer space, waiting to be corralled. Ideas exist in our own minds and we need to master the skilled techniques for bringing them forward for evaluation and application to our problems.

Brain-storming

One of the most favoured techniques for generating ideas is brain-storming. This is not the wild, undisciplined intellectual orgy that the name implies but a more systematic and proven method for arriving at some of the most likely solutions to a given problem or set of problems. In brain-storming, you liberate your mind and try to react without inhibition to your subject, allowing room for any and every idea that bubbles to the surface of your mind. The more ideas the better. Never mind the quality – just go for as many ideas as possible. The qualitative sieve comes later. Brain-storming comes with practice and simply helps to generate ideas.

Next, you need to sort out those ideas into groups, according to their usefulness. The test of the usefulness of an idea is whether it contributes much or anything to meeting two dimensions of any problem:

1. *The musts* An idea does not get past first base unless it meets the *musts* contained within the problem specification. For example, if I'm starting college and searching for somewhere to live, I might come up with a dozen possible ideas. But I've specified that the address *must* be within a half-hour's cycle ride from college and *must not* cost more than £*x* per week inclusive of heating and lighting. Any places that fall outside those parameters fail the *must* test and can be rejected, no matter how attractive they may otherwise be.

2. *The wants* Having satisfied the *must* test, every idea is then scrutinized to see how many of the *wants* it fulfils. For example, the initial listing of a dozen possible places to live has now been reduced to, say, six. And these six can now be further reduced by asking which of them meets a number of desirable but not essential *wants*: Which of them has a garden? Which of them is nearest to a bus route? Which of them is close to shops? And so on. By adding the pluses and minuses, it soon becomes apparent which of the remaining six places we ought to go to visit for a final decision. The final choice probably comes down to just one of the two remaining places.

Brain-storming is simply one of a number of 'thinking techniques' developed and popularized over recent decades to help us think more efficiently and creatively. Others include lateral thinking, straight and crooked thinking, potential problem analysis, rational decision-making, and so on.

If you begin to apply some of these techniques to your studies and make them part of your habits of thought, you'll find it much easier to solve problems, to write better essays and to produce higher-scoring examination answers.

SUGGESTIONS FOR FURTHER READING

de Bono, E., *de Bono's Thinking Course,* London: BBC Publications, 1982.
Thomason, J., *Critical Thinking Skills*, Columbia, South Carolina: South Carolina Educational Radio, 1988.
Stebbing, S.L., *Critical Thinking Skills*, Columbia: South Carolina Educational Foundation, 1988)

SOLUTIONS TO CRITICAL THINKING PROBLEMS

Problem 12.1
(Grateful thanks are expressed to Dr Julia Thomason of Appalachian State University, North Carolina, for this example, taken from her own creative work on critical thinking skills. See Suggestions for further reading above.)

The correct answer is twenty-seven boxes. If you have the answer as eighteen, you've probably forgotten to add in the additional boxes at each stage. The critical word here is 'each'.

Problem 12.2
The solution is UNDERGROUND.

There were two clues in the problem: first, that the letters had to appear in the same order, which helped you try out possible solutions; second, the word 'descend'.

Problem 12.3
The solution is A MAN, A PLAN, A CANAL: PANAMA.

The clues contained in the problem were the two commas and one colon. If you spotted that the word after the colon was PANAMA, the chances are you were soon able to supply the other missing consonants.

Problem 12.4
The surgeon may have refused to operate on the passenger because it was her own baby. The driver, in other words, was the surgeon's husband. If you had difficulty with this one, it may have been due to sexual stereotyping – i.e. you assumed the surgeon was a man.

Problem 12.5
The imaginative librarian first appeals for silence, to allow other students to get back to work. She then invites students A and B into her room to discuss the matter calmly. They soon agree that what they both want is a gentle current of fresh air, without direct draughts. She resolves the dispute by closing the library windows, opening all the windows in the rooms immediately adjacent to the library and propping open all the communicating doors. The librarian has applied critical and creative thinking, solving the problems to the satisfaction of all concerned.

13 Pass those exams – and stay human

> *Finals had been, in many ways, the supreme moment of
> his life . . . In the preceding months he had prepared
> himself with meticulous care, filling his mind with
> distilled knowledge, drop by drop, until . . . it was
> almost brimming over. Each morning for the next ten
> days he bore this precious vessel to the examinations
> halls and poured a measured quantity of the contents on
> to pages of ruled quarto.*
>
> David Lodge, *Changing Places* (1975)

This chapter tries to do three things:

1. To explain the reasons for exams.
2. To help you prepare intelligently for exams.
3. To help you improve your exam technique.

WHY HAVE EXAMINATIONS?

Exams are an inevitable source of stress. They represent the
culmination of a term or year's work or the end-point of a course of

study. They are in every sense of the phrase 'a testing time' – for students and examiners alike. So, what's the point of exams?

All colleges and institutions of higher education are required to carry out some assessment of student performance and potential. How does this student's work compare with that of fellow students in terms of quantity and quality of output? How does this student's work measure up to what teachers expect at this stage?

To answer such questions from potential employers or grant-awarding bodies (e.g. research institutes), teachers have to make assessments as impartially as possible. An 'unseen' exam paper allows different examiners to mark the same answers independently and to arrive at a fairly consistent and impartial assessment of the candidate's overall performance and potential.

At most institutions, the preferred method of assessment combines the marks obtained by students in 'continuous assessment' throughout the academic year with final examination results. By this means, a student who suffers badly from 'exam nerves' may benefit from having obtained good essay or project marks; conversely, students who dislike preparing written work on their own but who respond well under the time pressure of an 'unseen' exam may also do well.

Despite student impressions to the contrary, exams are not designed to set traps for unwary students. Rather, they aim to provide all students with the opportunity to demonstrate their knowledge of their subjects, their analytical skills and their capacity to handle complex issues under time pressure. So, if you've attended lectures, done the recommended reading, taken part in tutorial or seminar discussions, and completed your written assignments (paying particular attention to the constructive feedback given by your teachers), you have little to fear from examinations. But you still need to prepare.

HOW TO PREPARE INTELLIGENTLY FOR EXAMS

No athlete would dream of entering a big race without adequate preparation, both physical and psychological. You need to adopt the same approach to examinations. If you start your preparation too early, you'll reach peak fitness too soon. But if you leave your preparation until the last minute, you'll almost certainly panic and reduce your chances of scoring high marks on the day.

Only you can decide when to begin your exam preparation. The most important thing is to start in good time. If your exams are in May/June, you should certainly start your exam preparation by Easter. You can always take a few days off immediately before the exam to rest and refresh yourself.

TEN GOLDEN RULES FOR EXAM REVISION

Students study and learn in different ways. No one best way suits all students. We suggest ten golden rules for exam revision, but like all rules, they need to be interpreted flexibly.

Rule 1: take a positive attitude towards your exams
Start with the right psychological frame of mind. Remind yourself why exams are necessary (to measure student performance and to assess student potential), and why you are going to do well (because you've been reasonably conscientious and have prepared intelligently).

Rule 2: reduce stress and increase self-confidence
Make yourself familiar with the form of the exam. Most exams follow the pattern of earlier years. They nearly always offer a choice of questions, based on the syllabus that has been taught. Make sure there's no plan to change the exam format this year. Study past exam papers, noting the exam format, the choice of questions, and the all-important time limit. Examine the style and wording as well as the content of questions. Don't assume that questions will be worded in the same way every year. Examiners enjoy finding new way of asking old questions.

Rule 3: review your study material systematically
Go through your entire stock of learning materials (lecture, reading and tutorial notes, handouts, essays, newspaper cuttings, etc.), making a careful index under major and minor headings, with cross-references. Once you begin your revision, it's generally not a good idea to undertake new reading. Last-minute learning is often poorly absorbed and 'blocks' your memory.

Rule 4: revise actively, not passively
Revision means more than 're-viewing' or passing your eye across pages of lecture notes. Active revision means 'engaging' your material in a questioning approach: do you understand what your notes mean? Identify concepts, theories and writers. Follow up points you don't understand. Summarize your notes on cards under key headings and sub-headings. Revise from cards at odd moments.

Rule 5: learn how to retrieve and use your knowledge
Practise the art of retrieving ideas and making use of your knowledge. Learn to 'string' ideas together by making connections between concepts and theories from different areas. Use concepts across the

frontiers of knowledge. In that way, you get the best return on the time and effort you put into revision.

Rule 6: practise structuring effective exam answers
Good exam technique only comes with practice. Candidates who come to grief in exams often lack practice in structuring their thoughts into an effective exam answer. One page of well structured answer is worth ten pages of unstructured 'waffle'.

Rule 7: practise writing some complete exam answers
Get used to writing continuously for, say, forty minutes without a break. This helps you to develop writing skills and to manage your most important exam resource: time. Don't give up half-way through. Keep going. You can always fill in the missing details later. Be kind to yourself in judging your first attempts at answering exam questions under a time constraint. Don't panic!

Rule 8: don't daydream or drift into a negative frame of mind
Maintain good morale and keep fit during your revision. Remember to take regular breaks for fresh air, exercise and refreshment. Avoid excessive tea, coffee and alcohol. Take no drugs unless prescribed by a doctor. After a break, see whether you can capture the key points of the last topic you revised.

Rule 9: consider the value of co-operative revision
Most students revise alone. Some become anxious and depressed because they fall behind. Others find it best to work in a revision group. Tackling revision questions with fellow students reminds you that you're not alone; it allows you to comment constructively on one another's outline answers; it saves time; it is mutually supportive and helps you maintain good morale.

Rule 10: maintain a balanced revision timetable
Don't revise a few topics to the exclusion of all others. Spread your revision over two or more subjects each day. Take a day off now and then as a reward. Remember, you're building yourself up to peak performance on the day of the exam. Take regular physical exercise and get sufficient rest throughout revision.

HOW TO IMPROVE YOUR EXAM TECHNIQUE

Avoiding panic
Nothing creates more panic than arriving late for an exam. Allow

sufficient time to get there. Avoid anything that tends to increase your anxiety. Don't under any circumstances try to do last-minute reading. You'll simply 'swamp' your mind. Check that your writing materials, etc., are in good order. And use the toilet shortly before entering the examination hall.

Budgeting your time

Before the exam begins, listen carefully to the instructions given by the invigilator. As soon as the exam begins, check the instructions at the top of the paper to make sure that the format and duration of the exam have not been changed.

Budget your time according to your practice routine. If you're asked to answer, say, four questions in three hours, allow yourself sufficient time to study the exam paper and select the right questions for you to answer on that day. If all questions carry the same maximum marks, your answers should be given roughly equal time. In three hours (180 minutes), you can allow yourself a generous 5 minutes for reading the questions at the outset, followed by four answers of 40 minutes each (160 minutes), which still leaves a 15-minute margin at the end.

With 40 minutes per question, you might decide to allocate your time roughly as follows:

Thinking about the question   =   5 minutes
Structuring your answer   =   5 minutes
Writing your answer   = 25 minutes
Reading through your answer   =   5 minutes
Total   = 40 minutes

Selecting the right questions

Only you know which are the right questions for you to attempt. You might start by dividing the questions into three groups:

Group 1 Questions about which you know most and feel most confident. These are your target questions.
Group 2 Questions about which you know something but are perhaps not fully confident. This is your reserve group.
Group 3 Questions about which you know least and feel least confident. Discard this group.

In an ideal exam, you'll find your four favourite questions in group 1. If not, you should select them from group 2. If the exam paper is sub-divided into parts, make sure you answer the correct number of questions from each part, otherwise you'll lose marks, no matter how good your answers may be.

Decoding exam questions

Before you can answer an exam question, you must first 'decode' the
question to find what the examiners are 'driving at'. It pays to read
each question very carefully before you begin your answer. Many
exam candidates lose marks simply because they don't bother to read
the question carefully enough and therefore fail to answer the question
that's posed.

1. *Direct questions* usually begin with a command verb (e.g.
   examine, analyse, explain, outline, etc.). Remember to carry out
   the command. If you're asked to analyse some concept, it won't be
   sufficient merely to describe it.
2. *Indirect questions* often take the form of a provocative quotation
   you are asked to discuss. Beware of over-simplifying your answer.
   Honour the complexities of the question and try to show, by your
   answer, that you are aware of its many different facets.
3. *Multi-part questions* require you to do justice to all its parts. If
   you neglect, for example, the second part of a two-part question,
   you could lose up to half the marks for that question.
4. *The disguised question* is simply a familiar question in a different
   form. Many candidates don't recognize what the question is
   driving at. Their minds seem 'triggered' by some key word(s) in
   the question and they immediately plunge into an uncritical and
   largely irrelevant answer. You must penetrate the disguise and
   discover what the question is really about.

Structuring an effective answer

Having 'decoded' the question, allow your mind to associate freely on
the question for a couple of minutes. Then gather your thoughts,
perhaps using Buzan's starburst technique (see Chapter 9 on taking
notes from reading). Jot down quickly (in about five minutes) the key
ideas, concepts, authors, theories, etc., that you intend to use in
answering the question.

What you need is a simple but effective structure or framework,
strong enough to support the weight of your answer. The better the
structure, the more effective your answer. A good structure consists of
key words or phrases, not sentences, shaped into a coherent
framework on which to hang your answer. A good structure helps
your answer flow more logically. So you need lots of practice in
structuring effective answers. (see Ch. 11 for advice on structuring).

Writing an effective answer

1. Waste no time on preliminaries: you score no marks for writing

out the question – that simply wastes time. Every minute counts in an exam, so get straight down to your answer.

2. Approach the question logically and sensibly. Tackle the question directly and adopt a reasoned approach to the issues raised.

3. Give special attention to the first and last paragraphs and the first an last sentences of your answer.

4. Give your answer a strong conclusion. Many candidates simply leave their answer in mid-air. What's needed is a conclusion that pulls together the threads of your argument and rounds off the answer in a satisfying way. It should not simply repeat what's gone before or raise important fresh issues. It may be used to emphasize your key points. Above all, it should convince the examiner you've answered the question.

Scoring higher exam marks

What strengths do examiners look for in an exam answer?

1. *Comprehension* Has the candidate understood the question? If you don't show that you've understood the question, you can't answer it effectively.

2. *Relevance* Does the candidate stick to the issues raised in the question or wander off down by-ways? You score no marks for irrelevance or displays of peripheral knowledge.

3. *Analytical ability* Does the candidate reason his or her way through the question or simply muddle along its surface? Analysis means getting below the surface of the question.

4. *Expression* Can the candidate express ideas clearly, effectively and concisely? The length of an answer is no test of its effectiveness. A well-structured short answer is better than a weakly-structured long answer. Don't pad out your answer to make it seem impressive. Waffle is the examiner's bogey!

SUGGESTIONS FOR FURTHER READING

Main, A., *Encouraging Effective Learning*, Edinburgh: Scottish Academic press, 1981

Rowntree, D., *Learn How to Study*, London: Macdonald, revised edition 1976. Ch. 8.

14 Writing a research dissertation or project report

He had done his initial research on Jane Austen, but
since then had turned his attention to topics as various
as medieval sermons, Elizabethan sonnet sequences,
Restoration heroic tragedy, eighteenth-century
broadsides, the novels of William Godwin, the poetry
of Elizabeth Barrett Browning and premonitions of the
Theatre of the Absurd in the plays of George Bernard
Shaw. None of these projects had been completed ...
He ran hither and thither between the shelves of Eng.
Lit. like a child in a toyshop – so reluctant to choose
one item to the exclusion of others that he ended up
empty-handed.

David Lodge, *Changing Places* (1975)

This chapter tries to do three things:

1. To explain the purpose of a dissertation or project report.
2. To help you structure such a report.
3. To help you write and present a better report.

THE PURPOSE OF A DISSERTATION OR PROJECT REPORT

In the preparation of a project report, as in the organization of any other form of writing, structure is the function of purpose. You should, therefore, keep uppermost in your mind the principal purpose of your report. This is not just another essay, nor is it a PhD thesis. It is an opportunity for you to develop and demonstrate your skill in identifying, carrying out, and writing up a discrete piece of research, using the academic concepts, the theoretical insights and the practical abilities acquired on your course. This is *your* project. Unless you are a member of a joint research team, the results will represent entirely your own work and your examiners will judge it accordingly.

The secret of writing a successful dissertation (or project report) is preparation. In other words, you must have a good plan of what you propose to do and a realistic timetable from the outset. By keeping a sense of direction and watching your timing throughout the project, you reduce to a minimum the risk of last-minute panic.

Your first tasks are amongst the hardest: to clear your head and to get down to really thinking through the essence of your project:

1. What exactly is the problem or subject you intend to investigate? Unless you focus closely on the problem, you'll never succeed in your research or writing.
2. What are the main lines of enquiry you intend to pursue? You must think your way forward, cutting through the peripheral material, to arrive at the heart of your subject.
3. Identify your problem area and define your objectives briefly and coherently in written form.
4. Discuss these first written ideas with your project supervisor. To assist that discussion, you need to prepare three pieces of paper:

    (a)   A *one-page synopsis* or summary of the essential argument or line of investigation you intend to follow.
    (b)   An *outline structure* of the main sections of your report and the amount of space (i.e. the number of words) you intend to devote to each section.
    (c)   A *draft timetable* (which can be amended later) showing the dates by which you hope to progress your project from now until the date of submission.

Because your synopsis, structure and timetable are the keys to a successful project, they should be given priority attention. Sometimes it helps to produce two or three alternative structures, embodying quite different approaches to the same material. After reflection, you can select the best version or even combine the best elements from two or more versions.

STRUCTURING YOUR REPORT

Whatever the subject-matter of your report, your structure should ideally combine the following elements. (For reports in Science Engineering and Technology, see Ch. 11).

1. *Title page,* which specifies the title, author(s), for whom or what the report is submitted, date, department or place of origin.
2. *Table of contents,* which outlines the structure of the report and shows the page numbers of each section.
3. *Summary,* which provides a one-page synopsis, encapsulating the heart of the report.
4. *Introduction*

    (a) which explains what the report is about;
    (b) which provides a statement of the problem or subject of enquiry;
    (c) which says how you interpret the problem;
    (d) which indicates your approach to the task; and
    (e) which explains the lay-out of your report.

5. *Context*

    (a) which locates your project within a set of defined contexts (geographical, historical, economic, social, political, scientific, technological or combination);
    (b) which locates your project within a specific organization, where appropriate, delimiting those areas you intend to cover, those you propose to ignore – and why; and
    (c) which locates your project within an historical continuum and explains the time scale within which you carried out your empirical research (a chronology may be useful in an appendix).

6. *Review of literature*

    (a) which provides a summary of the main theories and arguments advanced by earlier researchers and writers in your chosen field of enquiry; and
    (b) which indicates the studies you intend to replicate, or the

theories you intend to rely upon, or the hypotheses you intend to test by your own research.

7. *Methodology*

    (a)   which describes the alternative methods you considered before deciding how to tackle the problem; and

    (b)   which says which method you finally adopted – and why.

8. *Research data or findings*

    (a)   which sets out the data you assembled during your research in sufficient detail to allow your reader to understand the analysis that is to follow; and

    (b)   which refers your reader to more detailed research data in the appendices to your report.

9. *Discussion or analysis of findings*

    (a)   which highlights what you believe to be the principal findings, usually in rank order of importance to you, or to the organization under investigation; and

    (b)   which interprets your findings and discusses their meaning and significance in the light of your prior knowledge and reading of the relevant literature.

10. *Conclusions/recommendations*

    (a)   which sets out in summary form the most important information derived from your research and the main lessons to be learned from your interpretation of that information;

    (b)   which spells out the policy implications of your findings and, where appropriate, the follow-up actions that appear to be necessary; and

    (c)   which indicates what further research might be undertaken to pursue some of the findings uncovered by your own research.

11. *Notes and references*

    (a)   which provide footnotes to material cited in the main body of your report (including author, title, place of publication, publisher and year of publication); and

(b) which elaborates important but subsidiary ideas that were too detailed to be contained in the body of the report.

12. *Bibliography,* which cites the principal sources on which you have drawn for your research, in alphabetical order of authors' surnames.

13. *Appendices,* which set out on separate numbered pages any detailed material, unsuitable for inclusion in the body of your report.

WRITING UP YOUR PROJECT REPORT

You should not think of starting to write unless and until you've completed four crucial preliminary stages:

1. *Thinking* about the meaning and content of your subject-matter and how you intend to approach the problem. This thinking should not be in abstraction but in writing.
2. *Researching* your subject to discover what other researchers have found before you. This takes the form of an 'academic literature search' and is often very time-consuming.
3. *Organizing* your ideas and your research material into some coherent line of argument or exposition. Students often find this the most difficult task: you have masses of material but now need to assess significance and establish priorities.
4. *Structuring* your material into an effective pattern that allows you to present your ideas as effectively as possible. At this point you should go back to amend your first draft structure before you start writing.

There is no 'one best way' to write up your project; we all have our tried and preferred methods (see Chapter 11 on better college writing). There is nothing wrong with starting in the middle or wherever you find it easiest to begin, but beware of leaving the most difficult sections until the end. You may well run out of time – or steam!

SUGGESTIONS FOR FURTHER READING

Phillips, E.M. and Pugh, D.S., *How to get a PhD*, Milton Keynes: Open University Press, 1987
van Emden, J., and Easteal, J., *Report Writing*, Maidenhead; McGraw-Hill, 1987

15 Fit for studying?*

Erst kommt das Fressen, dann kommt die Moral
(Food comes first; ideology comes later)

Bertolt Brecht, *Threepenny Opera*, 1934

This chapter tries to do three things:

1. To tell you how to feel great and fit for study.
2. To explain the importance of healthy nutrition.
3. To suggest ways to exercise sensibly and stay fit.

HOW TO FEEL GREAT AND FIT FOR STUDY

Health and fitness seem rather boring 'goody goody' subjects. Debauchery, let's face it, seems so much more exciting. But the

*This chapter was kindly contributed by Roslyn Taylor MA MPhil, Consulting Psychologist and Senior Partner at Lifestyler, a division of the Taylor Clarke Partnership, to whom any comments or queries may be directly addressed at 17 Grosvenor Terrace, Glasgow G12 0TB, Scotland (041-334 8686).

'bottom line' is that excesses lead to illness. What can be interesting is feeling more alive, having more energy and in general feeling great. Nutrition and exercise are the two keys to fitness and health.

Nutrition

Nutrition was not always the problem it is today. During the last war, for example, when people grew their own fruit and vegetables, when meat was rationed and anything sweet was in short supply, the nation was much healthier.

Today, the arrival of convenience foods with sometimes creamy fattening sauces, or hidden sugar, salt, fat and preservatives has changed our eating habits. The freezing and canning process reduces the number of nutrients in food. Fewer people grow their own vegetables or make their own soup. Opening a polythene bag or a can is the most we manage to do. And why bother baking a potato when a packet of crisps is to hand? The trouble is that though the fibre content may be the same, the fat content, which furs arteries, is eleven times higher.

At the same time, patterns of energy have changed. For example, we walk less than we used to as most families have cars and the launderette or the washing machine has replaced the scrubbing board. So energy output in general has been reduced. At school we may have been encouraged, even coerced into running around at sports. There is the danger that, when we get to college, this grinds to a halt when there is no one to tell you to do it. We shall return later to the benefits of exercise, but first, let's examine our eating habits.

Diets and dieting

Over-eating and over-drinking have become major problems for Western society. In 1983, research showed that in Britain 26 per cent of all adults were trying to lose weight, 35 per cent of all women. That's a lot of people, so as in the nature of things, dieting became big business with faddy diets and weight-loss systems abounding. There are creams to rub on offending areas, potato diets, banana and milk diets, grapefruit and egg diets, and very low calorie diets. The problem with these is that at the moment they end we say 'Thank God that's over!' and return to eating 'normally' – 'normally' being all the rubbish we ate before. Of course, the weight goes back on and we become human yoyos. We should not embark on diets if we are not prepared to change our eating habits for life.

A colleague, Sarah, recently graduated, decided to go on a very low calorie diet. She lost 4 stones (25.5 kg) in four months – too quickly by anybody's reckoning – and put all the weight back on, and more, in the ensuing four months. Her problem now is that her body has adapted to her starvation regime by slowing down her metabolism. Losing weight for Sarah is now a difficult task.

Changing your diet, rather than dieting, is a healthier alternative. There are changes we should all make (if we have not made them already) that have nothing to do with losing weight but are more to do with equipping ourselves for working at peak performance. It's a sad fact that machines are better maintained than bodies. A Martian viewing our race might wonder at our lemming-like ability to self-destruct by gobbling up nasty foods, smoking little chimneys and falling sideways as a result of consuming quantities of amber liquid. Complete *your diet questionnaire* to judge whether you need to make any changes in your diet.

Your diet questionnaire
Tick *yes* or *no* to the following questions:

                                                                Yes   No

1. Do you eat fried food as a general rule?
2. Do you drink some alcohol most days?
3. Do you sprinkle salt on your food?
4. Do you eat between meals, e.g. crisps and
    peanuts?
5. Do you take sugar in tea or coffee?
6. Do you eat sweets and chocolate?
7. Do you avoid eating vegetables?
8. Do you avoid drinking milk?
9. When you get uptight or depressed, do you
    put on weight?
10. Do you sometimes feel you will never become
    the weight you desire?

Any *Yes* answer denotes a vulnerability in your diet and ultimately your health. Let's discuss each point in turn.

1. *Frying food* increases the fat content, which adds to the waistline and the cholesterol intake. Coronary heart disease specialists advocate a diet low in cholesterol. Grilled, steamed or microwaved foods offer a far healthier diet.
2. *The occasional drink* can be beneficial and enjoyable but there are dangers. For a start, it's high in calories – about 180 calories per pint of beer, 80–100 calories per glass for a dry white wine. So, alcohol plays a part in obesity but in addition, physical and

mental performance are impaired. Concentration and decision-making are affected, more errors are made and the effects can be long-lasting. For every unit of alcohol (half a pint of beer; one glass of wine), it takes one hour to clear itself from the body. So, the effects of 4 pints of beer at lunch would take 8 hours to dissipate. Heavy drinking correlates with a number of physical conditions, e.g. hepatitis, cirrhosis of the liver, sexual difficulties, brain damage and high blood pressure. Vitamins are also affected. The current clampdown on drinking and driving has allowed people without embarrassment to ask for soft drinks at functions and market forces have led to an influx of low-alcohol wines and beers.

3. *Salt* in itself is not bad but in excess it stimulates the adrenals, encourages hypertension, arteriosclerosis and the retention of water in fatty tissue (cellulite). It also affects the kidneys, upsets hormonal balance and is mildly addictive. A sign of taking too much salt is if you find it difficult to remove the salt cellar from the table. There is sufficient salt for our needs in food already, without adding more. Try missing it out for two weeks and you will habituate to non-use.

4. *Eating between meals* supplies hidden calories. Often called 'dietary amnesia', half biscuits, peanuts, bits of cheese are eaten without the conscious knowledge of the consumer. Crisps, as discussed before, have a high fat content and peanuts, though good protein, are again high in calories and are often covered with salt. Thinking about food between meals, after meals or all the time predisposes snacking behaviour and over-eating. An obsession with food can be found in those who perhaps lead boring lives or, at the other end of the spectrum, stressed lives.

5. *Sugar* is 17 calories per teaspoonful. If, on average, a person takes 4 cups of tea/coffee per day, that is an extra 476 calories per week, or 24,752 calories per year. For someone who is only moderately active, that could mean a 7- or 8 lb (3- or 3.5- kg) increase in weight over a year. By the same token, if cut out, there would be the same amount of weight loss. To break the habit, try leaving sugar out of drinks for that magic two weeks. Most people find they cannot tolerate sugar after that period. Refined white sugar is also entirely lacking in nutrients and adds nothing to our diet.

6. *Puddings, sweets and chocolate* are very high in calories and, of course, sugar. Without totally excising them from your diet, it's advisable to cut down.

7. *Vegetables* are an excellent source of vitamin A, B6, E, C, minerals, protein and fibre. Be adventurous. Try different

vegetables to find out which you like. Remember, they will taste better than school cabbage.

8. *Milk* is a very important food. Containing protein, vitamins and calcium, milk is especially important for our diet if we wish to avoid osteoporosis (brittle bones) in later life. Whole milk contains fat, so a better choice that still retains the calcium content is semi-skimmed or skimmed milk. Other sources of calcium if milk does not agree with you are yoghurt, cheese, shrimps and ice cream.

9. *The stress response* in relation to being overweight is now being recognized by professionals. When stressed, we release cortisone into the body and this increases the appetite. Eating also has a relaxing effect, which is fine. But if this is your only way of relaxing then you may acquire a weight problem. For other relaxation techniques, see Chapter 18 on managing stress.

10. *Many people are negative* about their ability to control their diet. Self-disgust and guilt about over-eating maintain these cognitions. Learning to think positively and to look towards healthy outcomes can help considerably in any diet programme.

The balanced diet

For good nutrition and a balanced diet, first on the list is *protein*. Protein is made up of amino acids and forms all our cells – nails, hair, skin, blood, etc. Animal protein is good for us but may have cholesterol embedded in it – like fatty meat. Non-animal protein is better because it is low in fat and cholesterol.

Simple carbohydrates give us energy quickly, e.g. sweets, and sugar generally, but that energy is quickly dissipated. Complex carbohydrates on the other hand, e.g. pasta, release energy over a longer period of time. So, hunger is kept at bay longer. As a rule, we eat too many simple carbohydrates and not enough complex ones.

Fats are necessary for heat and energy. They protect the organs of the body and insulate us from the cold. But too much fat leads to obesity and heart disease. As in everything, 'moderation' is the watchword.

Fibre is essential in a diet to 'flush' us out. Potatoes, brown bread and cereals all help to this end (pardon the pun).

Vitamins spark the body into action. Since they are not produced by the body, we must get them from our diet and a deficiency in one can lead to an impairment in others. To get all these we need a balanced diet.

The daily food guide will help you plan your meals each day. And remember, you must eat these foods on a daily basis. An orange eaten on Monday will not supply you with Vitamin C until Friday.

A daily food guide
Meats Two or more lean servings daily. Count as a serving 3 oz (85 g) of cooked meat, fish or poultry. Use eggs, cheese, beans, peas, pulses and nuts as alternatives, if vegetarian.
Cereals Four or more servings daily. Count as a serving one slice of bread, half a cup of cooked wholemeal cereal or pasta and three-quarters cup ready-to-eat cereal. Use a whole grain or enriched product.
Fruits and vegetables Four or more servings daily. Choose citrus fruits, tomatoes, strawberries, or other vitamin-C rich fruit daily. Use dark green or yellow vegetables frequently.
Milk Two or more glasses semi-skimmed milk daily for adults. Three or more glasses whole milk daily for children. Four or more whole milk, semi-skimmed milk or skimmed milk for students.

Why a balanced diet is difficult to achieve
When we shop or eat out in cafés, college canteens or restaurants, we tend to select food for appeal and taste, not nutrient value. At the same time, we are often too busy to eat regularly, grabbing what is easiest rather than what is good for us. Then we wonder why we have no energy. The personal dislike of some foods such as vegetables, milk, liver, seafood (all good sources of nutrients) may limit a person's diet and lead to a depletion in a particular nutrient. Also, buying canned or frozen food rather than fresh food cuts down our vitamin intake by as much as 25–30 per cent. And it usually works out more expensive.

Even fresh food, if stored for long periods, will lose its vitamin content. Recently, in one supermarket, oranges were selected randomly, some juice extracted and analysed. Not an ounce of vitamin C did they contain. So, shop where you know there is high turnover of produce. The preparation of food can limit a balanced diet. When we cook potatoes or vegetables, we often scrape off the outer layer, which is most nutritious (i.e. the fibrous bit just under the skin), then boil off any remaining vitamins into the water, which is then poured down the sink. We literally throw our nutrition away. But if potatoes were cooked with their skins on, steamed or microwaved, carrots were scrubbed rather than peeled, and fresh fruit and vegetables chosen, then nutrionally we would be more equipped for living.

EXERCISE

When talking about nutrition as the input of calories to the body, outputs and calorie usage must be discussed. Digesting food uses up about 20 per cent of our calorie intake but the rest must be worked off by the energy we expend while living our lives. If these lives are sedentary then we risk becoming unfit and obese.

Advantages of exercise

The fact that exercise reduces stress is discussed in Chapter 18, managing stress. As a student, it's not always easy to avoid stress, so employing coping strategies is sometimes necessary. Exercise can burn up the adrenalin that worry, fear and frustration create, leaving the body relaxed and rested. After exercise you look good and feel good. A sagging body and a grey face do nothing for your confidence. Exercise stimulates blood flow to the skin and so gives rise to a healthy appearance.

Exercise, in addition to good nutrition, can guard against a whole range of serious ailments. The right kind of exercise can cure back pain, headaches and chest pain. Becoming more efficient at your studies is another side-effect of exercise, quite apart from reduced sickness absence from lectures and tutorials. Increased ability to concentrate and to make decisions has been shown to accompany the fit person. Exercise stimulates the brain so, in general, students who exercise regularly will look and be fit.

Five myths about exercise

Given the immense benefits of exercise, why do so many students try to avoid it? We tell ourselves that it's something we should be starting on 'one of these days'. Perhaps you were active at school but have now become active only in spectator sports; perhaps you have considered becoming more physically active but have lost your momentum before you ever began. Here are a few myths about exercise you might have believed in:

Myth no. 1: you have to be an athlete to exercise   At school, did you simply go through the motions in your physical-education class? Did you find the activities difficult and unenjoyable? Don't worry, there are many enjoyable physical activities in the 'real world' – activities that don't require special athletic background or 'natural' abilities.

Myth no. 2: exercising takes too much time   Do you have a hectic timetable and feel you just don't have the time to exercise? A regular exercise programme can require only 30 to 45 minutes, three times a week. In other words, one-and-a-half to two hours of exercise per week may be all that is required to improve your level of fitness.

Myth no. 3: playing 18 holes of golf or a couple of sets of tennis at the weekend is enough to keep you fit   Exercising once a week is not enough to make you fit. In fact, such spurts of exercise can be hazardous to a body that's not conditioned to handle sudden bursts of activity. You are more liable to injury when you exercise infrequently or irregularly. A weekly game of golf or tennis can, however, be an enjoyable part of a regular exercise programme.

Myth no. 4: exercise increases the appetite, so it can't help me lose weight Actually, the very opposite is true. Regular, moderate exercise helps regulate the appetite so that it more closely reflects your calorie needs. Exercise also keeps body fat from accumulating.

Myth no. 5: exercise will take too much of my energy and leave me exhausted If you're exhausted at the end of the day, you'll probably benefit from more exercise not less. Many students who exercise find that they need less sleep and have more stamina because their muscles can work harder and longer with less effort. Also, students who exercise regularly put less strain on their cardiovascular systems while accomplishing tasks.

To become fit – and stay fit – you must tackle three aspects of exercise: stamina, strength and flexibility.

Stamina – aerobic exercise Aerobic means with oxygen. Aerobic exercise is characterized by the body using large muscle groups in rhythmical continuous activity for relatively long periods of time. Examples of aerobic exercise are running, cycling, swimming, aerobic fitness sessions.

For the unfit individual, three times per week should be the maximum number of exercise sessions. Too much too soon causes injuries. Regular, enjoyable exercise is the key to fitness improvement. On the other hand, if you exercise less than twice per week, you are unlikely to make any noticeable fitness gains. Studies suggest that for improvements in aerobic capacity, you must raise your heart rate for at least 20 minutes per session. Initially some individuals will find it hard to keep exercising for 20 minutes because their joints and muscles are not accustomed to exercise. In this situation you should gradually work up to the 20-minute target. Finally, studies have shown fitness improvement levels off once you are easily able to exercise for 30 minutes. Therefore 30 minutes is a good target to aim for.

Strength – muscle conditioning Good muscle tone helps maintain stability of the joints and the postural muscles play an important part in a remarkable number of everyday tasks. The conditioning of muscles is, therefore, of importance to everyone but may be of additional importance to those who are interested in modifying their body shape through exercise.

Lifting weights or exercising in the college gym three times per week will help build strength. This may not, however, in itself provide sufficient aerobic exercise. I suggest this cautionary note as a result of personal experience. I worked out in a gym three times a week but when my fitness was tested for the BBC's *The Fitness Programme* (which, embarrassingly, I was presenting), it was discovered that although my biceps were passable, my heart and lungs were unaffected by my muscle conditioning. I was unfit. A relaxed jogging programme for 20 minutes, three times a week, for six weeks improved my fitness from just average to the 'high good' category.

Flexibility When your body is warmed up, you're physiologically more able to stretch the muscle ligaments and increase joint mobility. Regular and controlled stretching exercises will allow your limbs to operate through a greater range of movements with a much-reduced chance of muscle strain. You must be careful, however, to avoid excessive stretching. Five to ten minutes of stretching after exercise or attending a yoga class will help promote flexibility.

Now, write down the things you definitely know you do not like to do for exercise. There is space for five items, but you might have more. Make your categories specific. If you think you might possibly enjoy doing a particular exercise, but it is not something terribly exciting, do not write it down. This list is exclusively for things you definitely know you do not want to do, for example, 1. running; 2. swimming; 3. ski-ing; 4. toboganning; 5. karate.

Write down the answers to the questions listed below. Your answers will provide you with general categories of physical activities that are appropriate for you at this time.

1. Do you prefer to exercise indoors or out-of-doors?
2. Do you prefer to exercise with other people or by yourself?
3. Do you prefer to exercise in the morning, afternoon or evening?
4. Do you prefer to sandwich your exercise in along with your daily activities or to set aside time exclusively for exercise?
5. Do you mind having to change your clothing to exercise?
6. Do you mind getting your hair messed up?
7. Do you prefer to exercise in a gymnasium?
8. Do you prefer structure in your exercise or to do your own thing?
9. Do you prefer exercise that has a high level of excitement attached to it?
10. Would you prefer exercise that allows you to mark definite progress in your skill?
11. Do you like to have competition in exercise?
12. Is your preference to find something to enjoy, or just get the exercise finished and out of the way?

As a result of your answers, summarize your strongest preferences in Figure 15.1 taking into account stamina, strength and flexibility. Now commit yourself to a date to start, whom you will exercise with, and where you will exercise.

	Exercise type	Date	Partner/s	Place
1.	....
2.	....
3.	....
4.	....

Figure 15.1   Exercise schedule

In conclusion, if you can manage to balance your inputs and outputs, eat nutritionally and exercise regularly, your ability to study will certainly be enhanced.

SUGGESTIONS FOR FURTHER READING

Holford, P., *The Whole Health Manual,* London: Thorsons Publishing, 1988
Baker, J., *The Students Cookbook*, London: Faber, 1985

16 Tobacco and other addictive substances*

> *In a consumer society there are inevitably two kinds of slaves: The prisoners of addiction and the prisoners of envy.*
>
> Ivan Illich, *Tools for Conviviality* (1973)

This chapter tries to do three things:

1. To explain the most important facts about drugs.
2. To examine the effects of drug abuse.
3. To advise you how to get help on drugs.

*The information on which this chapter is based was kindly supplied by the staff of the Youth Enquiry Service, Strathclyde Resource Unit, the Scottish Community Education Council, and the Scottish Health Education Group to whom any comments or queries may be directly addressed at Adelphi Centre, 12 Commercial Road, Glasgow G5 0PQ, Scotland (041–429 2114).

THE FACTS ABOUT DRUGS

Drugs are used all the time in contemporary society. Some of the most commonly used, alcohol and tobacco, have the most serious effects on health. These drugs may be legal but, in the long term and short term, they can be dangerous. Even drugs developed for medical use can be abused. Drugs prescribed by doctors can be extremely hazardous if used in the wrong way. Everyday drugs, like aspirin, actually damage the stomach while curing headache. The less you rely on any drugs, the better for your health in the long run.

The pressures on young people – especially students – to use drugs are increasing. At college, you may find yourself being offered drugs. Don't be pressured into taking them until you know the facts. It's worth remembering that all drugs are open to abuse, and that people offer what they believe to be plausible explanations for such abuse: 'To escape my problems'; 'To relieve boredom'; 'To stay awake at parties'; 'For self-confidence'; 'To be one of the crowd'; 'To help me get on with people'; 'To stop me worrying'; 'To become more creative'; 'To help me study all night'; 'It blows my mind'; 'For a pick-me-up'.

Rather than helping them 'get away from it all', for many young people the misuse of drugs can add to their problems. Some begin by expressing the *need* for drugs; then become physically or mentally *dependent* on drugs and can't cope with life without them; some eventually become *addicted* to drugs. *Tolerance* means that with regular use, you need to increase the dose to achieve the same effect. *Dependence/addiction* are easily distinguished: we're all dependent on friendship, but we're all addicted to oxygen. You can live without the one but not the other.

Table 16.1   The effects of most commonly-abused drugs

Type of drug	Name	Effects/comments
Solvents (alter mood and perception)	Glue and solvents	• used mainly by under-15s • Produces excitement, loss of physical and emotional control • Risk of suffocation or choking on vomit • Risk of heart and brain damage • Sudden exercise while high can cause heart failure • High risk of accidents • Dependence is possible with some solvents

Table 16.1   Cont.

Type of drug	Name	Effects/comments
Hallucinogens (alter mood and perception, temporarily distort reality)	Lysergic acid diethylamide (LSD, acid, tabs)	• Alters the way user sees and feels things • Can cause confusion and panic • Dangerous to use on your own because effects are unpredictable • Long-lasting personality changes possible • Effects may recur in form of 'flashbacks' at any time up to two years later even if use has been discontinued.
	Psylocibin (magic mushrooms)	• Effects similar to LSD • Possibility of poisoning by eating wrong type of mushroom
Stimulants (speed up action of the central nervous system)	Amphetamines, (speed, uppers, pep pills, sulph)	• Feelings of alertness and anxiety • Suppresses appetite • High doses can produce illusions and disturbed behaviour patterns • Mental dependence can develop • Withdrawal can produce severe depression
	Cocaine (coke, snow)	• A brief feeling of euphoria • Mental dependence • Prolonged use damages inside of nose • Repeated doses causes anxiety and panic
	Nicotine (tobacco)	• Regular smokers find effects relaxing • Increases blood pressure and heart rate • Long-term smoking is linked to lung cancer and heart disease • Physical and mental dependence
	Caffeine (coffee, tea, soft drinks, chocolate)	• Makes you feel more alert • Large doses can cause anxiety and insomnia • Mental dependence can occur
Depressants (relax the central nervous system)	Opiates: heroin (H, junk, smack) morphine (M) codeine, opium	• Detached feeling of relaxation • Slows down body functions and reduces pain • Causes constipation and loss of sexual potency • Tolerance develops quickly • Physical and mental dependence • High risk of infection if injected • Withdrawal symptoms can vary greatly

Table 16.1   Cont.

Type of drug	Name	Effects/comments
	Cannabis (grass, pot, weed, hash, resin, black, shit, oil, leb, gold, blow)	• Intoxication like alcohol • Mental dependence • Risk of cancer if smoked • Risk of accident, especially if driving
	Barbiturates (barbs, downers)	• Reduces anxiety and tension • Causes drowsiness and loss of co-ordination • Physical and mental dependence • After-effects include insomnia, confusion and fits • High overdose risk especially with alcohol
	Tranquillizers (valium, librium, moggies)	• Reduces anxiety • Tolerance quickly develops • Physical and mental dependence • Can increase depression • High overdose risk especially with alcohol
	Alcohol	• Small doses reduce tension and relax inhibitions • Large doses lead to liver complaints and heart problems • Physical/mental tolerance and risk of accident

HOW TO GET HELP ON DRUGS

Using drugs can be dangerous, especially when they're taken in excess or for a long time, or in the wrong combinations. If you take drugs, you risk the following:

Overdose, which requires immediate medical attention
● An overdose can happen sometimes because the quality of drugs that are produced illegally vary according to how much they have been 'tampered' with to increase the profit to the dealer.
● It can also happen due to build-up of tolerance, when you need more and more of a drug to get the same effect.
● An overdose can cause mental disorders, fits, a coma or death.
● Overdosing of prescribed drugs can be fatal.
● Certain mixtures of drugs can be deadly, for example, alcohol plus barbiturates.

Dependence/addiction
- The regular use of drugs can lead to a mental and physical craving for them.
- Daily activities come to revolve around getting more drugs for the next dose. All other needs, even basic ones, such as food and friends, become unimportant.
- There is a narrow line between dependence and addiction. Although there are many personal difficulties to be overcome when attempting to withdraw from drugs, *it is possible*. Withdrawing from some drugs, such as barbiturates, are best dealt with in a situation where medical or specialist help is available.

Ill health
- Drug abuse can lead to damage to main organs of the body, mental illness, malnutrition or death.
- Drug abusers who inject themselves risk catching hepatitis (a serious blood disease) and many other infections, abcesses and even gangrene.
- Some drugs lower your perception of pain.

Accidents
- When drugs start to affect your mind, you will no longer be in control of all your actions. This is when you are likely to have an accident.
- You can become over-confident and take foolish risks. If you drive, you can injure or kill yourself or others.
- Unpleasant reactions during a 'bad trip' can make you panic and act irrationally.
- You may try to do things beyond your ability and get hurt.

If you use drugs you need to think about the following:

Legal problems
- The use of some drugs is against the law. If caught, offenders risk heavy fines or even imprisonment.
- Arrest can mean embarrassment not only for you but for your family and friends.
- It is difficult enough to get a job without having a criminal record.
- Some drugs can lead to people committing crimes or behaving violently.
- To drive under the influence of any drug is an offence – *and is dangerous*.

Money problems

- Continued use of drugs can be expensive, costing hundreds or even thousands of pounds a year. In order to pay for their drugs, many users get involved in crime including house breaking and male or female prostitution.
- Many drug users steal even from their own families and best friends.
- Drug trafficking is international big business and your money is their profit.
- To make a profit, drug dealers sell you short measures or mix all sorts of dangerous materials in with drugs to give them a bigger share of the profits or to finance their own drug habits.

Personal problems

- Relationships can be destroyed and friendships lost when you come to need drugs more than you need other people.
- Young people who abuse drugs regularly often end up as very immature adults because they never learn to cope with their problems.

Hurting others

- Arguments and problems because of drug abuse can lead to family disputes and breakdowns.
- Some people, when they have taken drugs, become violent and assault others.
- If you are pregnant, abuse of drugs could threaten your baby's health. The newborn child can suffer from physical dependence, withdrawal symptoms or even serious birth defects.
- Research has confirmed that women who continue to smoke and drink alcohol during pregnancy tend to produce smaller babies.

Drugs and the law

British drug laws cover many of the substances abused by young people. The Misuse of Drugs Act 1971 is the basis of the present drug laws. Anyone convicted of possession, supplying or producing drugs illegally could be imprisoned.

- The police have the power to stop and search anyone if they have reasonable grounds to suspect that person is in possession of a controlled drug. These powers of search without warrant also apply to vehicles.
- Police in the possession of a search warrant, signed by a justice of the peace or a sheriff, are authorized to enter premises, if

necessary by force. It is an offence to obstruct the police in their efforts to search for evidence of a drug offence.

● In the drive to combat drug trafficking, anyone found with even a very small amount of an illegal drug can be charged by the police with the offence of 'possession with intent to supply'. This charge automatically takes the case to a higher court, which can impose the highest penalties.

● Maximum penalties on indictment range from up to two years plus a fine for possession of class C drugs (e.g. mild stimulants, such as amphetamines) to fourteen years plus a fine for production and trafficking is class A drugs (e.g. heroin, morphine, cocaine and LSD).

What to do if someone takes an overdose

1.   If they become very excited or anxious:

   ● calm them down;
   ● prevent them from doing themselves an injury;
   ● don't leave them alone;
   ● if they don't calm down, call an ambulance or doctor (dial 999).

2.   If they become unconscious:

   ● put them in the 'recovery position' (i.e. on the floor, face down, but with head bent back and face tilted down, making sure they can breathe easily);
   ● call a doctor or ambulance immediately;
   ● if you can, give details of the drug taken when you phone;
   ● ask the ambulance operator if there is any first aid you can give;
   ● stay with them, until help comes;
   ● give them nothing to eat or drink.

How to recognize signs of drug abuse
Restlessness, exaggerated gestures, the appearance of being 'drunk', pinpoint or enlarged pupils of the eye, dowsiness, talkativeness or irrational behaviour.

Need help with a drug problem?
There are now many kinds of help available if you think you have a drug problem. If you are desperate, you may contact:

1. *a doctor* who will give advice and treatment and may refer you to a specialist drug-abuse centre for help;
2. *drug-treatment centres and clinics* who specialize in treating people with drug problems.
3. *hospitals* where treatment is sometimes given on an in-patient or out-patient basis;
4. *social-work departments* who offer practical help and advice and may refer clients to specialist helping agencies;
5. *Samaritans* who will always assist you to get the help that is needed. This is a 24-hour telephone service that helps anyone in despair. The phone number is in the phone book or may be obtained by dialling the operator; or
6. *college student counsellors* who have been specially trained to talk you through your problem and who may then refer to a specialized agency that can offer you help, at minimum disruption to your course of studies.

For further information, help or advice, contact your local regional health board, city health board, district health council or community health education group.

Their addresses and phone numbers are listed in your local telephone directory or can be obtained from the directory enquiries operator by dialling 192.

SUGGESTIONS FOR FURTHER READING

Leech, K., *What Everyone Should Know about Drugs*, London: Sheldon Press, 1983
Denham Wright, J., *About Drugs*, 11th ed.

17 Sex, love and dreams*

*Love between man and woman has many determinants,
but instinct is not one of them. Anthropologists have
described entire societies in which love is absent, and
there are many individuals in our society who have never
loved. To argue that such societies and individuals are
'sick' or 'the exception that proves the rule' (whatever
that means) is sheer arrogance. Love, when it exists, is a
learned emotion. Explanations for its current
prevalence must be sought elsewhere than in the genes.*

Lawrence Casler, 'This Thing Called Love is
Pathological', *Psychology Today*, American
Psychological Association, 1969

This chapter tries to do three things:

1. Examine sexuality and sexual relationships in the context of late
    twentieth-century college life.
2. Explore the concept of love and identify some of its pitfalls
3. Help you make sense of your dreams

---

* This chapter was kindly contributed by Yvonne de Barr, BA, a professional counsellor and
teacher of counselling to whom any comments or queries may be addressed, care of the author.

SEXUAL RELATIONS AT COLLEGE

If you've worked your way conscientiously through all the preceding chapters, sorted out the roof over your head, sussed out the teaching staff, discovered your way round the library and begun to develop good study habits, you may well be forgiven for thinking you won't find much time or space or energy left for anything like sex or love. Not so. Though the three or four years of your student existence will seem in retrospect to have flown by, one of the delights of this period of your life is the way in which the days – and nights – really do expand to let you fit in nearly all the things you want to do – and more!

There will be those who argue that you're really at college to learn French or physics or economics. That's less than half the story. You can and should 'learn to learn' and 'learn to live' at one and the same time. By combining these activities, you'll spend more of your life being a person than being merely a linguist, physicist or economist.

The first five years of life are critically important in shaping every person's unique individuality. So too are some other periods – like the one you're about to embark upon. You already know you'll be an intellectually different person at the end of your time at college. This chapter encourages a similar degree of growth and awareness in your sexuality and your ability to create and to sustain good sexual relations with others.

You may not believe it, but yours is a privileged generation. For your grandparents, sex was a taboo subject, enclosed by walls of 'Thou shall nots' and compounded by ignorance. For your parents, in those heady days of the 'swinging sixties', permissiveness was the buzzword. In practice, for most of us, neither of those places is a good place to be. The sexual pendulum has now swung back to a more central position, and that's good news!

The first thing to be clear about is that sex is a natural instinct: we are born as sexual beings. It's not a human characteristic which simply emerges at adolescence – though the changes associated with puberty tend to concentrate the mind powerfully on our sexuality at that stage. However, learning about your own sexual nature and how to express your sexual feelings don't just come naturally – despite what popular songs may say. The distinction is more clearly seen by analogy with breathing and eating: both are instinctive – yet, whilst nobody shows us how to breathe, learning to take sustenance is more problematic. Sex is more like eating than breathing in this regard – and interestingly, the word 'appetite' is often used in relation to both activities.

So, it's something we've got to learn about. Maybe all we need is a manual – 'Teach Yourself Sex'? No such luck: what makes sex much more complicated but also much more interesting and rewarding is that every single one of us has to learn what it's all about for ourselves – as unique individuals. Call it 'heuristic learning' or 'exploratory learning' or 'learning by doing' – that's the only way forward.

For some of you, the moral position will already be clear-cut. Your traditional culture, or your own religious beliefs, mean that for you, sexual experience, learning and growth will take place only within a monogomous relationship, probably within the institution of marriage. For others, the starting point will be very different – one night stands, so-called 'recreational sex'. Within our own dominant culture, probably more of the latter group will be men than women, though not exclusively so. Like other gender differences, this too is becoming more blurred as both sexes become more liberated – that is, more free to express themselves as individuals in ways that are right for them. Most of us, male and female, will find a place somewhere between the two ends of that continuum.

For all of us, the same general guidelines apply. They are not there to help us avoid heartache or hurt – that's not possible for real, alive, relating human beings. But, if followed, they will prevent us harming ourselves or others – not a bad guideline by which to live our lives.

The essential guidelines are simple:

1. You don't ever have to do anything you don't want to.
2. You should never be party to making anyone else do anything they don't want to.
3. And this is really important – you should never, ever assume that you know better than they, what they want – and never let anyone else persuade you that they know better than you, what you want.
4. You must keep within the law. Remember that the age of heterosexual consent is now 16 in England, Scotland, Wales and Northern Ireland – but it may well be different in some other countries. The age of homosexual consent (i.e. male homosexual behaviour in private) is now 21 in those four countries. But homosexuality is unlawful in some other countries. It's your moral and legal responsibility to find out what the law says and to comply with the law.

These guidelines don't mean you can't experiment and find out what feels right for you with another person. Indeed, it's the only way you'll ever find out. What it does mean, however, is that you retain the right both to say 'no' and to have that 'no' totally respected.

In terms of establishing what's right for you, you'll need to start by finding out about yourself. You didn't set out to drive a car without knowing where the clutch is and what it does. But successive generations of young people have embarked on their sexual experimenting without knowing very much about themselves – their own bodies, what turns them on, how they function sexually – and knowing virtually nothing about their partners. So examine, explore, get to know your own body first. Don't be misled by the ludicrous images in pornography and the media. You are you – there is no absolute to measure up against. And then read and learn about the structure of the opposite sex and the ways in which he or she functions. You may be fumbling in the dark – both literally and metaphorically – but you might as well know what it is you might find!

Next, before you find yourself in a situation you can't control you need to know about contraception and safe sex.

For there is a dilemma along the way – expressed so poignantly by the very young pregnant schoolgirl who, in response to the question: 'But didn't they tell you about sex in school?' replied 'Oh yes, they told me what to do – but nobody said how much I'd want to do it!'

All of you reading this book know how to think. Our society values thinkers and is quite good at training thinkers. But we're also emotional beings, with feelings as well as thoughts. Sometimes one aspect of our being has been developed at the expense of the other. In my professional work, I repeatedly have conversations with educated clients – especially male clients – which go something like this: 'Yes, yes – you've told me what you think, and what you did, but I wonder how you *felt?*' To which the response is so often a puzzled look and something along the lines of: 'But I just don't *know* what I feel'.

In your sexual relations with other people, you need to be aware of more than the behavioural aspects. You need to be in touch with the emotional content of the relationship. How are you feeling? And, just as important, how is your partner feeling? Fear, embarrassment, anxiety – all, if unacknowledged, get in the way of a real, live relationship. You need to be clear that for both of you what is going on is OK and creative of mutual satisfaction. And for that you'll need to talk about and share your feelings.

For the moment though, in the cool light of day, I'm asking you to apply your highly developed *thinking* faculty to the twin issues of contraception and safe sex.

Contraception

Once again, let's be clear. This is not just the responsibility of the female partner. Neither of you has any business bringing an unwanted 'out of time' baby into the world. The child and both of you deserve more than that. So, make an appointment at your family planning clinic or go and talk to your college doctor. It's never easy to decide these matters alone. But it's much easier these days to get the best information on which to base your decision. Make sure you do it now.

The actual choice of method is a very individual decision. What suits you may not be right for others. But remember, there's simply no excuse in this society, in the late twentieth century, for an unwanted pregnancy.

Safe sex

For sexually active people outside a long-term monogamous relationship, safe sex has always been important because of the danger of sexually transmitted diseases (STDs) – most commonly genital warts, syphillis and gonorrhoea. Untreated, there are unpleasant implications for you, for future partners and future babies. But, of course, they can be treated. Make contact with the so-called 'special clinic' (department of genito-urinary medicine) at your local hospital if you have any reason whatever to suspect that you may have contracted a venereal disease. All treatment is absolutely confidential and free.

It goes without saying – so we'll say it – that STDs are best avoided in the first place by routine sexual hygiene and precautions. If you're not sure what steps to take, go and talk to your doctor today.

What's highlighted the whole issue of safe sex is, of course, the advent of acquired immunity deficiency syndrome (AIDS). AIDS is different – because at this stage of medical knowledge, its treatable but not curable.

You become infected with the AIDS virus only through close intimate contact (involving an exchange of blood or semen) with a partner who is HIV positive – that is, carrying the human immuno-deficiency Virus that *may* develop, in some cases, into AIDS. And *only* in that way. Scares about glasses in pubs and communion cups are nonsense! Again, there's plenty of detailed information about – from your student union, from your local citizens advice bureau, from your college clinic. Once more, there's simply no excuse for ignorance. After all, you don't want to die of AIDS – either during or after your college career. Therefore, if you've been exposed to the possibility of infection and have puzzling symptoms, *see your doctor at once*.

If you have fears about being HIV Positive, see your college Counsellor. There are complex issues to be considered in relation to the virus and you'll need professional help and expert guidance.

A sheath (condom, johnny, french letter, 'Durex') plus a spermicide provides good protection for both partners against both unwanted disease and unwanted pregnancies.

Again, no excuses for being without – and that applies to women as well as men. You've only got one body: it deserves to be looked after.

Thus informed and protected you are ready – but only if it seems right for you – to embark upon a sexual journey that will last in one way or another for a life time. For most people, the best companion as you set out is someone you feel you know, someone you trust, someone you feel safe with. It's perfectly easy to take your clothes off – it's much harder to expose yourself emotionally, to render yourself vulnerable before another person – as you assuredly do in the expression of yourself and your needs in a sexual relationship.

You need to be confident, therefore, before you embark, that this is a good person for you to be with. That way, the sexual expression is part of the security of a genuine and preferably exclusive – though not necessarily permanent – commitment to each other. You may now have the chance of finding a sexual experience that involves not only the taking and/or giving of pleasure but one that involves you in 'sharing the experience of pleasure' in a meaningful way for both of you.

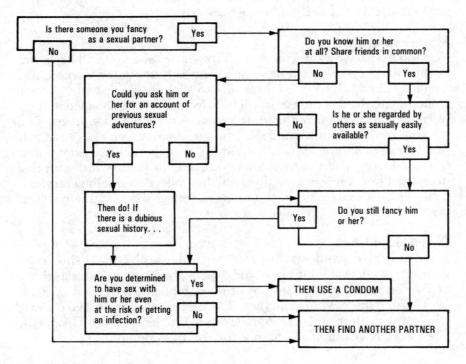

Fig 17.1   Play the safer-sex game

Homosexual and bisexual students

For a proportion of students – as for other groupings of adults – the partner will be a same-sex partner. For you, the journey is going to be tougher. In some countries, male homosexual practices are still illegal. In England, Scotland, Wales and Northern Ireland, where that is no longer the case, the age of consent for male homosexual behaviour in private is 21 and not 16 as for heterosexual relationships. (The law is silent on female homosexual behaviour.) You will undoubtedly encounter prejudice, hostility and misunderstanding. But my clinical experience tells me that for many of you, there's no choice – other than the possibility of celibacy – for as you've developed, you'll have gradually realised that your sexual orientation is homosexual and that you can no more change that than the colour of your eyes. For others, it will be less straightforward. The bisexuality within us all is presently unresolvable for you and it may take time to resolve itself. Homosexual (both gay and lesbian) and bisexual young people may find the going less tough in the company of an experienced counsellor. He or she won't tell you what to do – but will be alongside you (metaphorically) as you find your own way.

Mature students
You too may have a difficult path to tread. Around you will be young people, with few responsibilities and seemingly unlimited possibilities. You may already have commitments – to a family, to a partner. Those children and that relationship will be affected, will be changed in both obvious and subtle ways by your decision to become a student. The tensions can't be avoided and the ultimate outcome can't be predicted. But forewarned, the difficulties can at least be acknowledged and discussed. Again, if it becomes too difficult for you to deal with this problem alone, there are readily-available college counselling services. You've probably sacrificed a lot to get to college – don't let unresolved personal difficulties sabotage it for you.

Disabled students
Finally, disabled students also face particular problems. It should go without saying that your needs and expectations are the same as those of able-bodied students. But physical disabilities can make it difficult for you to express your sexuality. The best advice is to make contact with an organisation like SPOD (Sexual Problems of the Disabled). They have a wealth of experience for you to draw upon.

THE AGONY AND THE ECSTASY OF LOVE

In the hothouse atmosphere of college, there'll be lots of opportunity for 'falling in love'. The very phrase suggests a headlong dash – which is certainly what it feels like. There's not a lot of reason around when you fall in love. Often, in fact, you're responding to an unconscious pull towards that person which has little basis in reality. What seems to be so compellingly attractive in that person is often a 'projection' of a repressed part of your own personality. So the quiet, reserved, studious girl falls 'head over heels' in love with the most outrageous extrovert in the year! Hardly surprising that it often 'ends in tears'. While it lasts, of course, it's both ecstasy and agony: totally obsessive – every waking moment – and some dreaming ones – full of him and her; delightful fantasies of what might perhaps be the actual realisation of some of those fantasies. All this puts you in touch with the core of your 'feeling being'. Enjoy it while it lasts. You'll look good, you'll feel good, and you'll have masses of energy as the adrenalin flows!

Two warnings:

1. If you find you never get beyond the stage of 'falling in love' or 'being in love' and meeting the other as the real-life individual behind the projection, then you may need some help to look at what's happening and why.
2. If you find in the longer run that the process of 'being in love' stops you functioning properly (i.e. getting your college work done) that too is something you might need to look at with some skilled help (i.e. a skilled counsellor).

'Being in love' and 'being loved' are naturally the next stages. By now, the fantasy has somewhat abated and some reality has entered the relationship. You relate as two real adults who probably share values and attitudes, enjoy many of the same things, doing them together and who care about the well-being and happiness of one another. And have lots of fun. But it's not all plain sailing. After a while, it may emerge that the man's experience and the woman's experience of that closeness are somehow very different. For it sometimes seems that men and women inhabit different emotional worlds. The conventional wisdom would be that 'men are independent, women rather more dependent'. Emotionally, nothing could be further from the truth. And we don't need to look far for the explanation.

As children, we all need a significant adult on whom we can truly depend: in our culture, for both boys and girls, that person is likely to be a woman, usually the mother. Men therefore learn to expect that their dependency needs will be met by a woman (now a mate rather than a mother but a female none the less).

But what about women? They are essentially, though not necessarily explicitly, raised to be 'depended upon' – to meet the emotional needs of others. (Why else are so many women in the caring professions?) So, in essence, in order that the partnership can really start working emotionally for both partners, they must jointly seek to develop within the male partner the ability to nuture, and within the female the ability to recognise her own needs and to ask for them to be satisfied. That all requires a considerable degree of maturity, honesty and commitment. Now you see why I said that sex was the easy bit!

Next come all those variations on the theme of love which are intrinsically full of pain as well as pleasure:

- Love which, for whatever reason, is destined to remain forever undeclared.
- Love which is unrequited: however much you love somebody there's absolutely nothing you can do to 'make' them love you. Nothing: that's a particularly poignant kind of pain.
- Love which is not going to be fulfilled. Circumstances, many and various, may mean there's no way forward for that relationship. Often, two individuals will sadly suffer their pain and loss alone, unable to share either the love or the suffering.
- Love within a partnership in which, for one of you, the love is still there and yearning to grow and develop, whilst for the other, it's gone, it's over, it's finished.

All this, of course, falls within the range of normal experience, as you move through your early adulthood. A very heady brew in the atmosphere of most colleges.

Each experience teaches you something more about yourself, your own needs and what you have to offer others. And each experience helps you to mature emotionally.

Danger signals arise when the normal pain and unhappiness that accompanies all emotional growth enlarges to become a depression which you simply cannot shift, particularly if you feel (for more than a passing moment) that there's nothing left to live for – or if you realise in time that you've stopped being able to look after yourself. At that stage, you *must* tell somebody how you feel: a fellow student, a tutor, a lady in the canteen – somebody. Talk about your feelings with them and that will help you decide if you're going to need some professional help to come through this experience which is very common and in which you can be helped, no matter what you may feel at the time. There is help available: we all need at some stage to avail ourselves of it. It's just your turn this time!

And there may be those of you reading this who have a friend or colleague suffering in that way right now. If so, you'll be wondering what you can do to intervene, to ease the pain. What your suffering friend needs at such a time is to have you just listen, not to judge or to find the answer but to offer practical support if necessary. But above all, just to 'be there' for them. Don't forget, you may need them to be there for you, another time, another place!

MAKING SENSE OF YOUR DREAMS . . .

From the pain of love . . . to the world of dreams. No, don't turn over, those of you about to say: 'But I don't dream'. You do, in fact, dream, for up to one fifth of the time you're asleep. You just haven't developed the capacity to recall those dreams.

Being at college is a time of great activity for you – intellectual development, physical growth, psychological insight – so it's also a time when you may well experience particularly vivid dreams. Wild dreams, troublesome dreams, Technicolor dreams. Don't ignore them as an avenue for self-discovery, for growth. Freud called dreams 'the royal road to the unconscious'. So, if you really want to know what you're feeling and thinking in this new world of college, why not try to catch yourself dreaming?

First, there are different sorts of dreams. For both men and women, there are erotic dreams – with feelings of acute arousal which for men (less often for women) may sometimes culminate in involuntary orgasm ('wet dreams').

Then, as students, you may be familiar with 'the examination dream' – of sitting and taking an examination or a test which you've already taken and passed. Perhaps an additional reassurance that you can in fact pass your future examinations!

Other types of dream worth mentioning are:

Traumatic dreams – which involve the reliving of some trauma – such as an accident, a mugging, or a sexual assault. No need of explanation here. These dreams usually fade in time and then die away. Importantly, they may in fact be helping you come to terms with the traumatic experience.

Anxiety dreams – which again need little explanation. We've all had such dreams – in which we find ourselves wearing the wrong clothes, in the wrong place, at the wrong time, missing the train, etc. Anxiety is part of our daily life. However, constant experiencing of anxiety dreams might suggest a waking life out of balance, a need for some adjustment. (See also Chapter 18 on managing stress.)

Recurrent dreams – with which many of us are familiar. These dreams are usually evidence of some unresolved problem or dilemma. The imagery might be such that you can work it out for yourself (e.g. always in pursuit of a partner but never quite catching him or her!).

Wish fulfilment dreams – they're the ones where you actually get to catch that partner – useful of course if you hadn't previously acknowledged to your waking self who it is you're pursuing in your unconscious mind!

Finally, of course, come nightmares. Strictly speaking, these refer to dreams where you are pursued and eventually overpowered by a monster. More commonly, the term is now used to describe any really frightening dream. Nightmares are not normally experienced by adults in good health, though we may all experience one occasionally. If you find yourself prey to regular bad night terrors, it might be worthwhile talking the problem through with a counsellor, trained in dream analysis, to look at the imagery and try to discover what the messages are for you, what your fears are all about.

So, how can you work with your dreams in such a way as to make useful links between your conscious and your unconscious mind, and so gain some benefit in your everyday life?

1. You have to recall the dream. On waking, try staying in bed for a few minutes and let your mind try to recall. Don't force it – let it do the work. Most people find they can improve their recall of dreams with practice. It's mostly a question of wanting to do so!
2. Keep a pen and paper by the bed (or a tape recorder). Try to record anything you can remember – details, a feeling, colours, even an odd word can sometimes trigger the total memory of a dream.
3. When you've captured your dream, what then? Certainly not a routine interpretation of certain symbols attached to specific meanings. Your dream is a personal experience. Only you can look for associations, explanations and seek amplification of what it was your unconscious mind was trying to communicate to you while you slept – and dreamed.

By investing some time and trouble in learning to capture and interpret your own dreams, you may well gain insight into those aspects of your life that we've been discussing throughout this chapter – some of your needs as living, loving, sexual being, surviving, as we all must, in complex relationships with other people.

SUGGESTIONS FOR FURTHER READING

Cousins, J., *Make it Happy*, London: Virago. 1973
Comfort, A., *More Joy of Sex*, London: Quartet Books, 1988
Webster, L., *Dream-work: Guide to the Midnight City*, Dryad Press, 1987

18 Managing stress*

*Rid me of my Devils – but do not
rob me of my Angels*

*Words believed to have been addressed
to his psychotherapist by the German
poet Rainer Maria Rilke when seeking
help during a severe depressive illness.*

This chapter tries to do three things:

1. To explain the sources of stress.
2. To examine the effects of stress.
3. To provide an action plan for stress-proofing.

*This chapter was kindly contributed by Roslyn Taylor MA., MPhil, a consulting psychologist
and Senior Partner of the Taylor–Clarke Partnership, specialists in motivation,
communication and stress management, to whom any comments or queries may be directly
addressed at 17 Grosvenor Terrace, Glasgow G12 0TB, Scotland (041–334 8687).

THE SOURCES OF STRESS

Contemplate your day – today or yesterday. Were you annoyed, frustrated, angry or depressed at any time? If yes, then you were probably under some degree of pressure. Pressure can be beneficial, even motivational. To progress in any way demands some form of pressure.

So when does pressure become stress? The question itself exerts some strain on the writer because this transition point may be different for everyone reading this chapter. One person's stress is another's stimulation. Witness parachute jumping or hang-gliding – surely stress-provoking for the sane and sensible? In general, stress consists of demands made upon us that exceed our ability to cope. These demands can come, for example, from the environment, a domineering parent or a possessive relationship. They can also arise from within ourselves.

Internal sources of stress
The desire to reach perfection in all our undertakings is unrealistic and yet so many people have this perfectionist philosophy when selective adequacy is often sufficient. We can also create problems by being hard-driving and competitive whereas a more relaxed approach can be just as successful. In the USA in the 1960s, an upholsterer registered amazement to two clinicians that it was only the fronts of the waiting-room chairs that needed renewal – the backs were virtually untouched. He asked what they did to their patients that had them sitting on the edges of their seats. Next day, the two doctors spied on their patients and sure enough the majority were poised as if expecting an imminent departure.

The two clinicians were Friedman and Rosenman who had been researching the causes of coronary heart disease. The upholsterer's observations changed the course of their research. They began to look at stress as a major cause of heart disease and their research revealed two behavioural types: A and B.

Type A people tend to accept more work than they can cope with. They are the ones who are hard-driving, competitive perfectionists and are often impatient and aggressive if thwarted. On the other hand, type-B is characterized by complacency, low output, disorganization and a total lack of pressure. Do you recognize yourself – or bits of yourself – in these descriptions? You should aim for a balance between A and B. Work hard but take some time off to do nothing.

In the USA, the use of relaxation techniques is being researched for use in business. Researchers have already found, for example, among advertising executives that concentration and decision-making are significantly improved using these techniques. The time taken for such a group to produce a creative package for a company advertising scheme was cut to one third of the usual time.

Learning how to relax will make your time at college more fruitful. You can do this by purchasing a relaxation tape and using it systematically (two to three times per day) for three weeks. To form new habits or break old ones, three weeks' practising the new behaviour is all that it takes but it must be *continuous* practice.

Yoga classes and meditation are also beneficial, especially if you prefer an inter-personal flavour to your relaxation. Another benefit of the 'course' or 'class' approach is a commitment to attend, having paid a fee. You need to be motivated to keep practising on your own.

This kind of 'natural' relaxation is infinitely preferable to smoking, drinking or taking drugs of any kind. Although you might imagine they help you unwind, they actually stop you reaching a relaxed state of mind. Drugs and alcohol tend also to eradicate REM (rapid eye movement) sleep. If you have ever watched someone sleeping, their eyelids flicker occasionally while they dream. This is REM sleep and if diminished by alcohol or tranquillizers, etc., it may leave you feeling 'drained' and lifeless, as if you have hardly slept at all.

External sources of stress

An example of an external source of stress is change, and the transition from school to college is possibly one of the biggest changes anyone can undergo. You may not leave home, but you will certainly change your social circumstances, your working conditions, your financial situation and probably your beliefs and values. That makes for a lot of change.

Psychologists and physiologists tell us that even 'good' changes like winning the pools (or a lottery), moving to a better home or getting married (a little dubiety on the latter) can affect us detrimentally. We lose concentration, may become disoriented and can even suffer illness or accident.

Human beings are often in conflict over change – they hate being prised from their rut but, at the same time, seek change to add spice and stimulation to an otherwise humdrum existence. Balancing the two responses is a lifetime's challenge.

College examinations are another stressor with the implication of failure (see Chapter 13 on pass those exams – and stay human). Nothing can engender rabid anxiety and pessimism like a bout of the 'end-of-terms/semesters' or a dose of 'finals'. Anxiety and pessimism do seem to be linked because it is our negative thoughts about ourselves and our performance (or lack of it) that produce anxiety. Concentrating on positive outcomes rather than ruminating on the negative could help enormously. If you were asked to recall the best thing that ever happened, you might have difficulty. But if you were asked to recall the worst event, the chances are a specific situation would come instantly to mind, the details in lurid Technicolor, words and phrases intact.

To change, you must focus on positive outcomes: on success not failure. Anticipatory anxiety – that sinking feeling you experience prior to an event – is thus reduced and life is less stressful. Easy to say but hard to do. To change your thinking style takes dedication and effort: you must be aware of every negative thought and then replace it with a positive. Keep the following questions to hand during a 'down' spell and try to make your negative thinking more objective.

Questions to challenge negative thoughts

- What evidence is there to support your negative thoughts? For example, are you really a total failure or have you just failed in one area?
- Are there any alternative explanations of the event that are not negative?
- How might someone else react in the same situation?
- How does negative thinking stop you from reaching your goals?
- Can you react differently?

Many students cope well with exams but find that relationships or the lack of them provide distress and despair. Tom, a student in his final year, had worked to the exclusion of all else. Then he realized that in his year social groupings had formed and many students had paired off. He, on the other hand, became increasingly isolated and began to generate a philosophy of human nature that was selfish and uncaring to explain his situation. His negative thinking led to suicidal despair and he was referred to a psychologist. Ultimately, he forced himself to go into social situations, had to convince himself that he was worthy of friendship and began to see his studies as less overwhelmingly important.

THE EFFECTS OF STRESS

If stress is prolonged and intensive, then lasting psychological and physical damage may occur. The human body has the technology to cope with mental and physical pressure. Adrenalin is produced and blood flow leaves the peripheral bits – hands, feet, etc. – and moves to heart, lungs, brain – all to help us get through the crisis. What the body is less able to cope with is prolonged pressure or anxiety coming from perhaps more than one source. When this happens, the body's resources become depleted and illness may result.

A music student of my acquaintance suffered habitually from 'flu-like' symptoms immediately before a performance. These symptoms were very real to her and did not appear to be brought on as an escape. She did, however, become nearly hysterical at the thought of failure nearly two weeks before the concert and under stress her body literally let viruses in.

Ulcers, high blood pressure, coronary heart disease – even some cancers – often have stress as a precursor. Post-viral syndrome thrives on stress. Stress depletes the body of vitamins, especially the B and C vitamins. Illness can result, further destroying bodily resources and it may be months before recovery is complete.

As well as attacking physical well-being, stress can affect us psychologically. Poor concentration, poor decision-making and difficulties in memorizing are all associated with stress. Performance in all sorts of situations can be profoundly affected. During my own final exams, I noticed that a friend who had shown signs of anxiety seemed to be working very industriously, rarely pausing, like the rest of us, to summon inspiration. Gradually I became aware with my peripheral vision that she was writing her name continuously and had been doing so for three hours. This is an extreme example of stress where the person becomes dazed, disoriented and regresses to a very simple level of responding.

Without adding to your stress, it is worth being aware of these damaging effects. Symptoms appear as the body tries to adapt, so recognition of these signs is a major step in counteracting stress.

Checklist of signs of stress

Study the checklist in Table 18.1 to identify any signs of stress in yourself. Tick any of the symptoms you have experienced. If you score a total of more than three ticks, then you may have to work out what is causing your stress – whether *internal* (i.e. are you causing it?) or *external* (i.e. is something or somebody else causing it?). Then look at the action plan for stress-proofing and choose one of the techniques that might suit you in your situation. If the symptoms continue, speak to a doctor or counsellor at the student health service.

Action plan for stress-proofing

- Learn to relax with yoga, meditation or a relaxation tape. Not only will it relieve stress but also the effects actually improve performance with better concentration, memory, decisions and creativity.

- Become a positive thinker. Cynicism and sarcasm, especially when turned on oneself, are destructive. Positive thinking is not naïve but an ability to 'look for the good'.
- Create a support system in your year that allows you to discuss options and solutions to problems, especially personal ones.
- Spend time on some interests not related to your course.
- Exercise regularly. It helps to release tense muscles, can induce relaxation and provides a sense of well-being.
- Review your aims and goals. You may need to change direction as you change as a person.
- Cut down on smoking and alcohol. Remember, they stop you becoming totally relaxed.
- Make sure you are eating a diet balanced in protein, carbohydrates, fats, vitamins and fibre. Low-calorie diets are dangerous and do not give sufficient energy for an active life.
- Reward yourself for success. Treat yourself to something out of the ordinary – be it a meal or a music tape, etc. (grant permitting). Alternatively, stop occasionally to say, well done! Don't forget, you are always more critical on your own performance than any friend, colleague or examiner. So catch yourself doing something right for a change!

Table 18.1   Checklist for signs of stress

Physical	Mental	Behavioural
Headaches	Inability to relax	Awkward body positions
Indigestion	Irritability	Poor posture
Insomnia	Loss of sexual desire	Fidgeting
Palpitations	Poor memory	Pacing up and down
Tiredness	Poor concentration	Restlessness
Chest pain	Intolerance of noise	Always rushed
Diarrhoea	Over-reactions	Fast speech

Remember also that pressure can be productive. Your best work may be achieved prior to a deadline or during an exam. This chapter does not oppose that view. On the other hand, stress is more destructive and must be controlled to keep it within safe limits.

SUGGESTIONS FOR FURTHER READING

Cooper, C.L., Cooper, R.D. and Eaker, L.H., *Living with Stress*, Harmondsworth: Penguin, 1988

19 Money matters*

NO MONEY STOP NOT FUNNY STOP YOUR SONNY
TOO BAD STOP HOW SAD STOP YOUR DAD

(Anon.)

This chapter tries to do three things:

1. To explain the special services most banks offer students.
2. To offer hints on student budgeting and possible savings.
3. To suggest how to cope if expenditure exceeds income.

WHAT MAJOR SERVICES DO BANKS OFFER STUDENTS?

Most – but by no means all – students will receive some form of financial allowance during all or part of their studies. Whether that allowance comes in the form a grant cheque or parental contribution,

*This chapter was kindly contributed by Alwyn James MA, Chief Press Officer, The Royal Bank of Scotland Group plc, to whom any comments or queries may be directly addressed at 42 St Andrews Square, Edinburgh EH2 2YE, Scotland (031–556 8555).

the amount of money in your purse or pocket is invariably larger than anything you've carried around before. So it's quite difficult to resist the temptation to spend that money quickly, even recklessly. Remember, however, that this money is intended to support you throughout the whole of the term until your next 'top-up'. And don't forget that the vacation will also make demands on your pocket. The most useful first step is to open a bank account so that you can deposit your grant cheque or parental contribution.

Which bank?
When you arrive at college, you'll find you've become a very important person as far as the banks are concerned. In their wisdom or otherwise, they believe that today's student is tomorrow's prosperous customer and, as most of us are reluctant to change banks, it's important for their new business that banks should attract young people at the very point at which they decide on their bank. This is a decision that often stays with them for life.

The result of that thinking is that you'll find yourself on the receiving end of many very attractive-sounding offers. These vary considerably from year to year and indeed from bank to bank, so the decision on how you react to these blandishments is yours. It's impossible to evaluate all the banks' offerings, particularly as they're likely to change each year, but let's look at some typical offerings in 1988–9:

1. *The come-on* Here are three examples. Ask yourself how important each might be to you:

    Bank A 'Open an account with us and you can enter a competition offering chances to win one of 50 Transalpino return rail tickets to Rome, 75 tickets to Amsterdam or a copy of a Europe by Train handbook'.
    Bank B 'Open an account with us and we'll give you a £20 cash gift, on receipt of your first grant or parental contribution'.
    Bank C 'Open an account with us and we'll give you £12 cash credit or £10 cash plus a free National Express/Citilink Student Coach Card (which normally costs £3.90 and gives you a one third discount for a full 12 months)'.

2. *The financial incentive* Different banks offer cash credits or differing amounts paid into your account immediately you sign on – even before your grant/contribution is paid in! Again, some typical examples:

Bank A £15 cash plus free draw tickets;
Bank B £12 plus free gifts; and
Bank C £20 cash but no gifts.

3. *The banking service* Once again, different banks offer a bewildering choice of service including the following:

- Immediate but limited cash credit.
- Current or deposit (with cash-dispenser card) account.
- Interest-free overdraft of up to £200 + where agreed in advance; or preferential interest rate (e.g. 1 per cent over bank rate) on first £250 of agreed overdraft.
- Commission-free travel facilities – e.g. travellers' cheques, foreign currency.
- Waiver of issuing fee of £7 per card for a Eurocheque Card.
- Free banking – i.e. no bank charges levied on accounts that remain in credit or that do not exceed the agreed overdraft.
- Immediate cheque guarantee card to facilitate payment for goods or services by cheque.
- Cash-dispenser card enabling you to withdraw cash from a network of cash-dispensing machines covering most of the country.
- Special possessions and contents insurance.
- International student identity card (which normally costs £4 and which provides various discounts both at home and abroad) where bank is able to direct mail to new students through the college.
- Financial assistance to parents (whether or not currently the bank's customers) of up to £7,500 at preferential interest rate of 2.5 per cent over bank rate for a period of up to three or four years.

These and many other elements will enter into your decision when choosing a bank, for example, which branch is most convenient for you? Location has become somewhat less important with the ready availability of cash dispensers – but you may still want to talk over your money matters with the bank manager from time to time.

Find out which bank your college itself uses. The bank may well offer college staff – and students – special discounts. In short, it pays to shop around for your financial services.

What type of account?

Once you've decided on your bank there's another decision to be made, which type of account do you want to open? The decision is a personal one but your chosen bank will be able to advise you. There are two basic accounts:

1. *The current account*, which is by far the most flexible as it normally offers a cheque book, cheque guarantee card and cash-dispenser card. Armed with a current account you can write cheques for goods and services; with a cash-dispenser card you can obtain access to money around the clock, providing of course you either have enough money there to take out or that you have arranged for a suitable overdraft.

    The disadvantage of a current account is that you receive no interest on your money – although if most case histories are to be believed, very few students have significant amounts in credit to earn any worthwhile bonus from this source!

2. *The deposit or savings account*, which pays you interest but you will not receive a cheque book. The account is normally available with a cash-dispenser card so that the availability of cash either from a machine or through passbook from a branch is no problem.

It's worth noting that you should be able to use your cash-dispenser card at any one of a number of different bank machines, depending on which group of banks you are with. Group A includes: National Westminster (England and Wales only); Midland; Northern; Clydesdale; TSB (Scotland only). Group B includes: Barclays; Lloyds; Bank of Scotland; Royal Bank of Scotland.

HINTS ON STUDENT BUDGETING AND POSSIBLE SAVINGS

Until now, for most of you, the budget was some national event involving an elderly gentleman, an even more elderly briefcase and excessive television coverage. Now, perhaps for the first time, a budget is something with intense personal significance. You should work out as early as possible a budget that will give you a clear indication of just how much you have to spend throughout your time at college. The equation is not a complicated one (even for the non-mathematically minded). Here are some of the steps you'd be well advised to follow:

1. *Work out* exactly how much money you will receive for the term/semester – rarely a difficult task! In most cases, it will come from either or both of two potential sources – the local-authority grant and the parental contribution.

2. *Add up* your estimated expenditure for the term/semester. In most instances, you'll have a very clear idea of just what the costs are going to be. Some costs – such as lighting and heating, books and equipment – will be less easy to estimate in your first term/semester. Make sure you've included an adequate amount to cover rent and/or any other accommodation costs, fuel, lighting, heating, food, travel (including occasional fares home, if appropriate), books and equipment and a contingency allowance.
3. *Deduct* your total estimated expenditure from your total income to find out what, if anything, you have left over for personal expenditure.
4. *Divide* this figure by the number of weeks in the term and the vacation and you'll find out just how much (i.e. how little!) you have to spend each week. If you've much left over, you're a very lucky and unusual student indeed!

Possible savings
The cost of accommodation will, of course, depend on where you stay (see also Chapter 2 on accommodation). Halls of residence may seem expensive at first but remember that you only pay during term time and the cost usually includes a lot of items such as heating, lighting and some meals – all of which can mount up horrendously on top of what at first may seem quite reasonable charges for staying in private-sector accommodation (e.g. a flat or shared apartment). Again, it's worth remembering that very often you'll have to pay for a flat or lodgings all the year round or throughout certain of the vacations.

Fuel, lighting and heating are, as mentioned earlier, usually included in the fee for halls of residence but if you're in a flat, do try and cut down on unnecessary use. You'll be amazed how expensive it is to have a couple of degrees of extra warmth, and how much cheaper it is to buy a warm sweater than to put on an extra bar of the electric heater. Again, hours spent studying at the library rather than at the flat may not only be more conducive to the acquisition of knowledge, it may also contribute significantly to a reduction in your electricity bill.

Food is inevitably a large item in every student's budget. If you're in self-catering accommodation, it's cheaper to share the cost of food bills with your flatmates. Shop around for the best buys. Work out whether a safari once a month to a distant hyperstore offers any significant savings. Remember that many fruit and vegetable traders and some local food-store managers reduce the price of perishable foodstuffs just before weekend closing (usually around 5pm on a Saturday). Eat in college refectories where the food is nutritious (though perhaps boring) and often cheaper than more glamorous city restaurants.

Books and equipment are often inescapable items of expenditure. Their cost will vary considerably depending on your course of studies. You may save money by purchasing reasonable quality second-hand books from other students, from the college bookshop or the student union. Many college libraries will stock multiple copies of the books most in demand. Enquire before you lay out scarce cash!

A contingency fund may seem an unduly pessimistic provision or an unnecessary luxury, but it's always best to allow for the unexpected expenditure that may arise – a pricey book you just can't manage without; a field trip; that irresistible night out; or an unexpected need to return home. These are just the sort of hiccups that can ruin your budget.

Why budget?
It's extremely important that you budget your money sensibly. If you don't you may find yourself running out of money towards the end of term. Since this is the very time when you're studying hardest for exams, your poor budgeting could put your academic career under severe strain.

An overdraft is a fact of college life that few, if any, students manage to avoid. At some time during their studies, most students will need to take out of the bank more than they have put in. The most convenient way of coping with peaks in the demand on your finances is to arrange an overdraft with your bank.

The first thing to understand is that there's a big difference between an overdraft and becoming overdrawn. An overdraft, in essence, is an agreement from your bank that you'll be allowed to take out more money than you have in. The Royal Bank of Scotland is more than a little proud and proprietorial about the overdraft. They claim to have invented it in August 1728 and say it's proved one of the most imaginative and flexible means of borrowing. The fact that it's still around, 260 years later, indicates something of its value.

The overdraft offers the means of ironing out that rather erratic graph that indicates the unpredictable demands on limited money. At the same time, it's a fact of life that very few students can make do on the money they receive from various sources and banks are keen to help their young customers through this difficult period. They're often accused of making credit too easy for young people and getting them into an early habit of living in debt. But if banks were to withdraw overdraft facilities tomorrow, there would be chaos in the colleges of Britain – and not only amongst students!

The first step is to go to your bank to try to arrange for an overdraft facility. Most bank managers will be sympathetic to your needs and, as part of the student package, you'll very often find that your overdraft charges are lower than those made to any other category of bank customer. Again, it's fairly common for banks to waive any service charge when you go into overdraft – something your contemporaries who have gone into employment instead of higher education will not be favoured with!

Two final lessons:

1. If you know your parents (or anybody else) has agreed to pay some money into your account, let the bank know before you start drawing cheques up to that amount. *You* know there'll be deposits to cover those cheques – but don't assume the bank knows!
2. If you run into financial difficulties, the earlier you go to your bank manager, the more open you can be with him or her about your position, the more likely you are to get his or her wholehearted support. But don't try it on too often!

SUGGESTIONS FOR FURTHER READING

For students in England, Wales and Northern Ireland: National Union of Students, *Welfare Manual*, London: NUS, annually
For students in Scotland: University of Strathclyde Students' Association, *Welfare Manual*, Glasgow: USSA, annually
All the banks publish their own information booklets: e.g. National Westminster Bank, *Student Information Pack*, London, annually
Trustee Savings Bank, *A Student Account*, Edinburgh, TSB, annually.
Royal Bank of Scotland, *Threshold: a comprehensive guide for students*, Edinburgh, Royal Bank of Scotland, annually.

20 Students facing special problems*

All happy families resemble one another, each unhappy family is unhappy in its own way
Leo Tolstoy, *Anna Karenina* (1875–6)

This chapter tries to do three things:

1. To explain why certain students face special problems.
2. To identify six groups of students with special problems.
3. To suggest ways in which students may help themselves.

THE MAJORITY

The vast majority of students survive and succeed at college by overcoming the problems that typically face all students: the lack of decent accommodation; shortage of funds; the stresses and strains of

*This chapter was kindly contributed by Craig McDevitt, MA, Senior Student Counsellor, University of Edinburgh, to whom any comments or queries may be directly addressed at Student Advisory Services, University of Edinburgh, Scotland (031–667 1011).

examinations; personal relationships that don't always run smoothly; difficulties of communication with the student's family; and so on. But whereas nearly all students have some passing acquaintance with these problems, there are six groups of students for whom these problems are compounded. Let's deal first with the majority.

The majority of British students are in the 16–24 age group. If you fall into this age group, you're going through a very important period of your emotional development as a human being. This is the transition between adolescence and adulthood. It's a time of change – and change always means the loss of what you're leaving behind and the excitement and fear of what you're moving towards. Such a mixture of feelings can cause confusion and most people can't stand feeling confused. So, you will spend a lot of time and energy trying to keep confusion at bay. That's why you'll find yourself being very interested in finding out the meaning of life, the world, the universe – and everything! Questions such as, 'Who am I?' What am I doing here? Where am I going?' will never be far from your mind and certainly central to what is known as the 'existential crisis'. This will probably be the first time you've experienced this crisis – but it certainly won't be the last!

Given that the majority of students are in this period of transition with its attendant preoccupations, it's quite surprising that any academic work gets done at all! Colleges usually recognize that students are undergoing an emotionally-confusing period that can interfere with studying. For that reason, you will probably find that your college has a student counselling service where you can go to talk about your problems and, with the help of a trained counsellor, find solutions of your own. Generally between 5 and 10 per cent of all students in your college will see a counsellor in any one year.

Nobody is immune from having problems, it's in the nature of being human. There are, however, some groups of students in every college who are likely to have more difficulties because they are in some way(s) different from the majority and/or are subject to prejudice from – and perhaps discrimination by – the college community. Such students might find it difficult to integrate fully with the college community, which would be unfortunate, given that the key to happiness at college often lies in being able to integrate successfully. There are six such groups, which we now deal with in sequence.

MATURE STUDENTS

If you are older than twenty-four and starting college, you will fall into this category. Although increasing numbers of mature students are now enrolling in colleges, you still form a minority within the college. Age not only separates you from the younger students but also from each other because mature students come from very different backgrounds, experience and preoccupations. Some are single, some are married, divorced, separated, widowed, with families or without. At first sight it might appear that you have little in common with other students. Even if you do have something in common, you've little time to spend with other students when other demands are placed on you outside college.

A common fear amongst mature students is that the bright, young, teenage students have much more agile brains and that consequently you will perform poorly by comparison. It's true there's some deterioration in short-term memory as one becomes older, but the decline is pretty insignificant. A real difference between you and younger students is that they are often more practised at studying than you. For many mature students the real academic struggle is more to do with maintaining self-confidence. Many of you will have come late to college precisely because your earlier educational experience was less than happy. If that's the case for you, it's important to remember that the bad experience was most likely to do with unfortunate circumstances rather than your own poor ability. After all, if you didn't have the ability to survive and succeed you wouldn't have been accepted into college.

Another issue that you might have to struggle with is disappointment with college life. Many mature students come to college with very high expectations of themselves and of the college experience. Coming to college may have been seen as a way of changing your life or enhancing your career prospects. There are times (hopefully not too many) when college life is dreary and a drudge. The subjects you've chosen to study might seem to have little obvious relevance to your chosen career, if you have one. This is a common experience amongst mature students and one that is worth talking about to a student counsellor.

Finally, in my experience, mature students put a lot of pressure on themselves to get things right and to succeed. This may be because they feel they owe it to their families who are making sacrifices to enable them to come to college or they are being subsidized by employers, or because they feel it is their last chance to succeed. It might even be because they are older and therefore feel they ought not to make mistakes. This can make it difficult to acknowledge to others that all is not going well. It's important to remember that being older does not necessarily mean being able to cope any better than younger people (which refers not simply to students but also to staff!).

DISABLED STUDENTS

If you're a disabled student you will be well aware of the limitations placed on you by your disability. To some extent, the college authorities will also be aware of these limitations – because they took them into account when you were selected for college entry. Having got that far, you will have overcome some obstacles but it's possible that further limitations will emerge in the course of your studies and if that happens, you and the college will have to negotiate a way through.

More important perhaps is the extent to which your disability will prevent you from enjoying full participation in student life beyond studying. Some barriers might be impossible to overcome and you will have to come to terms with the pain of that realization. To overcome other barriers, you might need the co-operation of your fellow students. Gaining sufficient acceptance from your fellow students to elicit help can be a difficult task and one in which you will have to play an active part. From past experience, you'll know of the wide range of negative responses your disability evokes amongst the able-bodied. Your fellow students might feel uncomfortable with you or even afraid of you*. Some might ignore you, act as if you were feeble-minded or overcompensate by becoming too eager to please.

Ultimately it is you who will have to help them to see you as any other human being with similar feelings, wants, interests and impulses, even though your disability might mean that you have special needs. You will have to make these special needs known to others. This is not always easy to do because you will have to do the asking and because the able-bodied take so much for granted.

Once you have gained the co-operation of your fellow students, you will have made friends and be well on the way to becoming integrated within the college community.

OVERSEAS STUDENTS

The first few weeks of college are not usually difficult for overseas students. Many colleges will make an effort to ensure that you are made welcome and besides, it can be very exciting to come to a new country. Once the official welcomes are over, however, and the reality of having to work in this new country emerges, many of you will begin

*I recall to this day with shame that throughout my undergraduate career at the LSE in the mid-1950s, I was unable to bring myself to talk even once to a fellow student, a young Israeli, whose face had been severely disfigured by wounds received in a tank battle. He coped brilliantly as a student. It was I who was emotionally handicapped and unable to cope. (S.M.)

to realize what you've left behind and what lies ahead for you. Like most students you're having to handle changes and their resultant losses, gains and confusions. However, unlike other students from Britain, you will be handling very major changes.

Some of you will be leaving wives, husbands or children behind. You'll also be leaving a familiar culture and climate (not to mention places and friends) for an environment that's strange and unfamiliar. You might be struggling with learning, writing and operating in a language that's not yours and of which you still do not have total command. Even if you're fully proficient in English, you might find the different regional accents of English difficult to understand.

In this confusion of new things it's very important to be able to adapt to the new environment and begin to feel at home. A major priority will be to find a place to live where you'll be warm and comfortable and feel that it's a little piece of home ground to retreat to when you are tired of struggling with the strangeness of British food, British weather or British people!

Another major priority will be to make contact with other people so that you will not feel isolated. Not all British people will welcome you with open arms. That might be because some people might feel hostile towards you because of your country, culture or race – but more often than not it's because British people are rather reserved and shy about making friendships quickly. An additional and very good reason for making friends with a few British is that your new friends will be able to explain to you something about the culture and customs in the UK. The burden of adapting to the British way of life is very much on your shoulders. To gain acceptance, you'll have to learn to do things the British way. However, I would advise you not to become too British because your foreignness will make people interested in you and want to get to know you.

Because a great deal of your time and energy will be taken up with trying to adapt and to become comfortable with the new environment, you must not expect too much of yourself in your first year here. (It often takes a full year to become comfortable in a new place.) It's to be expected that your ability to study will not be as good as it usually is when you're back home. This can make many overseas students feel anxious because they often put a lot of pressure on themselves to do well, feeling that the opportunity to study in Britain is a privilege – one that will give them increased prestige and enhanced career prospects back home. To fail would, therefore, be humiliating. There's no doubt that to be seen to fail would cause you pain but it would also be sad if your memories of living in Britain were unpleasant. So, do take time to relax and to enjoy yourselves.

BLACK STUDENTS

It would be foolish to pretend that there's no racism in British society. If you've grown up here, you will have met both blatant and subtle forms of prejudice. It would be an invidious form of prejudice to assert that it makes no difference if you're black. As a black person, you'll have been through experiences where you'll sometimes want to respond differently from a white person. To deny these differences would be to deny your identity as a black person, living in a predominantly white society. Additionally, if both black people and white people do not recognize such differences, we all run the risk of not being able to reach an understanding of each other. At the same time, it's important to recognize that, black or white, we are more alike than unalike, first and foremost because we share a common humanity and second, because on campus at least, we share a very similar college experience.

Although colleges are supposed to be places of enlightenment, neither staff nor students will be entirely free from prejudice. It can be very difficult to confront subtle forms of prejudice but blatant discrimination should simply not be tolerated. There are the provisions of the Race Relations Act to help support the fight against discrimination. If you feel that you're the victim of discrimination or harassment at college, you can call initially on your student union to advise and support you if you wish to take any action against such behaviour. If you fail to achieve satisfaction, they will advise you where to go next.

WOMEN STUDENTS

Despite the tremendous changes concerning the equality of women in British society over the past twenty years and more, there's still a long way to go before men and women are treated as genuine equals. In my more optimistic moments, I feel it will take several generations for attitudes to really change because the attitudes that support inequality are frequently transmitted from parents to children in very subtle and unconscious ways.

Being a part of society, colleges are no more free from sexual discrimination and harassment than anywhere else. Look around you at your college! How many professors or senior lecturers are women? What's the balance between the sexes in your classes, especially in such traditionally 'masculine' subjects as engineering? Is there a blatant or subtle difference in the way in which staff treat women and men?

Think about your choice of subjects. Have you been gently steered towards traditionally 'feminine' subjects that might in turn lead to suitable 'feminine' careers?

As with black students, it can be difficult to challenge the subtler forms of discrimination, but it's important to become aware of them in order to maintain your autonomy, to share your experience with others and to help create a better understanding with the possibility of change. However, the more blatant forms of discrimination should certainly not be tolerated and sexual harassment is one of the most intolerable forms. It may be very crude or highly subtle, and it's unfortunate but true that female students and female members of staff can experience sexual harassment in college. If you feel you're the victim of harassment, it's your right to protest, to be listened to and responded to by the college authorities. It's not always easy to pursue such a protest because you might be distressed by the victimization or find it difficult to prove. You might also find that the authorities try to minimize things by suggesting that you are over-reacting or that you in some way provoked unwelcome attentions. If you're in any doubt about making such a complaint or finding it difficult to pursue one, get in touch with your student union. They have a commitment to sexual equality and will therefore offer advice and support. If you have the strength to pursue a complaint, you are helping others in the long run. In addition, the college authorities, who have the power to reprimand staff members and students, need to be made aware of the extent to which harassment causes great distress, anger and confusion and can put students' academic work at risk.

GAY AND LESBIAN STUDENTS

How you feel about being gay at college will depend very much on how far you've been able to acknowledge that you are gay. Some of you might be well aware of your sexual preference for people of your own sex, be open to others about this and active in the search for satisfying sexual relationships. Some of you might only be at the stage where it's just beginning to dawn on you that you are not attracted to the opposite sex or even attracted to both sexes. Some of you might have already acknowledged to yourselves that you're gay but are anxious about coming out and telling others because you fear hostility, rejection or ridicule from friends, fellow students or parents.

It's important to recognize that no matter where you are in acknowledging your sexual preferences, you're not much different from most other students of your own age in that they, too, are struggling with their sexuality. The importance of realizing this is that it's all too easy to feel a freak if you have gay feelings. This is because homosexuality is not much talked about – apart from the usual jokes – and that society is still not fully accepting of homosexuality. We also know that a lot of people feel anxious about homosexuality because they're afraid of their own homosexual feelings. It can be a comfort to remember, if you feel a freak, that nobody is 100 per cent hetero– or homosexual. What makes us choose our own sex, opposite sex or both sexes is how predominant our hetero– or homosexual preferences are.

It would be false to claim that being gay brings no difficulties. Some people will be negative in their reactions and refuse to see beyond your sexuality and recognize your personality. You'll have to come to terms with this. On the other hand, you'll experience to the full the joys and the pleasures (as well as the pain) of relationships with lovers, gay and straight friends, if you feel comfortable about being openly gay.

Many colleges have lesbian and gay societies and it might be useful to join such a group as it will provide you with the opportunity to discuss and explore the issues that arise from being gay. Joining also helps to combat the feeling of being the odd person out. After all, you can't know if people are gay just by looking at them. Lastly, being a part of a gay student society helps to maintain your identity as a student. Many gay students can feel isolated in the student community and become alienated when the only opportunity to express their gayness is by socializing in off-campus gay bars and discotheques.

Finally, a last word to all students. For all students, but especially to those students who are in some way different from the majority, an important key to being happy and successful at college is the feeling that you belong. People come together because of mutual interests and a need for support. If you belong to any of the six groups mentioned above, you'll probably find that there are groups existing to suit your special needs and interests and consequently you may benefit from joining. One of the benefits is that groups are almost invariably more powerful than individuals and therefore offer a greater potentiality for bringing about changes in attitudes and policies in the college community. If there is not a group to suit your needs, you might find it most rewarding to start one. You'll find you're soon joined by others!

SUGGESTIONS FOR FURTHER READING

Consult your College or University Student Services Department, Counselling Service, or Student Advisory Service.

21 Where to go for advice and help

*Ask and you will receive; seek and you will find; knock
and the door will be opened.*
Matthew 7,7, *New English Bible*

This chapter tries to do three things:

1. To explain why nearly all students need some help and advice.
2. To suggest how you should go about getting such help.
3. To suggest how to make best use of such help.

WHY DO STUDENTS NEED ADVICE AND HELP?

Sooner or later, nearly every college student seeks help and advice with
some taxing problem they've encountered during their college
experience and which they cannot cope with alone. The problem need
not necessarily be grave or even serious. It may concern health or
money or studies or accommodation. Whatever the nature of the
problem, it's one that the student does not feel confident of handling
alone. There's no shame attached to seeking help.

On most college campuses, help is at hand. Over the years, college administrators have found that students regularly need help. Each college has explored ways of helping its students to get back to their studies quickly and at least cost by offering them some form of immediate help on campus – sometimes called student counselling, or student advisory services, student medical services or whatever. If the problem is really serious, for example, a severe illness, students can then be quickly referred to more specialized or advanced agencies for further advice and attention.

HOW SHOULD YOU GO ABOUT GETTING SUCH HELP?

When you've no money ...
Down the centuries, as reported throughout a worldwide literature search, students have always been proverbially short of ready money. There may be a grant on the way, or a cheque from home in the post or part-time earnings to come at the end of the week, but, just for the moment, your average student is broke.

The first person to see is your bank manager or your building society manager, if you have one. They were probably students themselves not long ago and may be sympathetic to your situation. They may extend credit or offer advice on how to get some (see also Chapter 19 on money matters).

If you still fail to solve your money problem, you should certainly go to see a student counsellor at student advisory services (or whatever name is used locally). Money problems nag away at your sub-conscious, reminding you that you are insolvent and that, in turn, affects your concentration and your ability to study successfully. Most colleges have an emergency fund that is available to help students with short-term financial difficulties, not of their own making. It pays to enquire about such a fund. You will never know what assistance may be available unless you ask.

When you've nowhere to stay ...
Having nowhere to stay is often connected with having no money. Good student accommodation becomes increasingly more difficult to find in our congested towns and college cities, but no student should ever have to sleep rough – for more than a night or two, at worst (see also Chapter 2 on accommodation).

You should certainly report your difficulty at once to the student advisory services staff. They've a great deal of experience in dealing with such problems and may be able to help you – or even offer you short-term accommodation on campus, until you can find yourself somewhere more permanent. You should go today, the earlier the better. Don't leave it until the evening, when the office is closed and there may be nobody on duty who can help you.

When you're feeling ill ...
We all know what it's like to wake up feeling out of sorts. If you've been to a party and over-indulged in food or drink, there are usually common remedies to hand. If you've caught a chill and ache all over, the best thing may be to stay in bed for the day and take an aspirin with hot fluid every hour or so. If you're feeling really bad, you should certainly try to let somebody know, so that they can keep an eye on you. You may recover of your own accord – but you may need qualified medical attention.

If you feel ill on campus, there's often a student health service available during normal working hours. That may include an emergency dental service. Alternatively, there may be emergency nursing staff to offer you help and advice until you can get to a doctor. In dire emergencies, there's always the casualty department of the local hospital. But do check in advance that your local hospital has a casualty department – many have been closed in recent years.

If you think you may be pregnant and need help and advice, go to see the nursing officer on duty today. Don't leave it until tomorrow. If you think you may have contracted a sexually transmitted disease, there's no time to lose. Go to see the nursing officer on duty today. If you develop persistent symptoms, such as bleeding or severe pain, seek urgent medical advice today. Do it now. Tomorrow may be too late!

When you're feeling lonely ...
Most students are gregarious creatures who seek and find pleasure in other people's company. Wherever you come from, whatever your subject, you'll normally find it easy to make contact with fellow students at the student refectory or the student bar or coffee shop. But you won't want student company all the time.

There may come a time when you're feeling down or out of sorts when you don't want to talk to another student. You're disappointed or distressed about something in life – an emotional problem perhaps, a financial problem, a work problem or some other personal problem you'd rather not share with another student (see also Chapter 20 on students facing special problems).

Once again, there's usually some qualified and experienced person you can go to talk to in complete confidence. Begin with a student counsellor or student advisory services. They may be able to help you themselves or they may refer you to some other person, even better qualified to help you. Alternatively, there may be a chaplain (minister, priest or rabbi) on campus, who will be ready with guidance and advice, if you need it, or simply offer you a sympathetic ear and a cup of tea. Don't let small niggling problems reduce your working efficiency. Don't be too proud to seek help. Go to talk your problem through, in confidence, with a professionally-qualified adviser, and do it today.

When you can't cope with your study ...

If your problem is clearly study centred, the best person to advise you may be your class teacher, subject tutor or personal counsellor. Most students run into some learning difficulty, at some time during their course of study. It may be you can't get hold of the key books or articles you need for a written assignment. It may be some difficulty with understanding a technical point in the literature. The problem may be associated with cognitive learning (an intellectual blockage) or affective learning (an emotional blockage) or it may be a combination of the two. Whatever it is, you need help. Don't fret and lie awake at night. Go to see your teacher, tutor or counsellor tomorrow morning. If he or she is not there, go to the department office and try to make an appointment. Tell the department secretary the degree of urgency, so that he or she can pass the message on quickly, if necessary (see also Chapter 3 on students, teachers and other college staff).

When you can't cope with people ...

There may come a time when you simply can't face your fellow students or your teachers or your room-mate. Nobody in fact. That's a symptom reported by many students from time to time. You may need to be alone to get your life into better perspective. You may be physically exhausted; you may be unwell; you may simply be mentally stale and emotionally drained. If so, take a break from your studies for a day or two. Don't begrudge the missed lecture or seminar. But drop a note out of courtesy to your tutor or counsellor explaining your proposed absence. If the weather allows, get out into the countryside. It needn't cost a fortune. Try joining the Youth Hostel Association (telephone number in *Yellow Pages* phone directory) and take advantage of relatively cheap overnight accommodation. Get some fresh air and oxygen into your system and you'll generally find you sleep better and your normal appetite for life will soon return. If you give yourself a day's strenuous walking, make sure you're properly equipped with map and compass and suitable all-weather protection. And tell a trusted friend where you're going.

If you still can't cope with other people when you return, make an appointment to see a counsellor at student advisory services. If there's something preying on your mind, explain your feelings simply and clearly to your counsellor. There may be some problem blockage which prevents you from working or from being normally sociable. There's no shame attached to such feelings. Talking by itself won't necessarily solve all your problems, but it certainly helps most students to find their equilibrium again.

When you're in trouble with the law ...

Each year, a small number of students at nearly every college seems to fall foul of the law. It may be something as simple as a parking offence or as serious as an eviction order from your digs. But it might be much more serious: an alleged offence concerning drink or drugs or antisocial behaviour, with a prosecution pending.

Whatever the problem, don't try to be self-sufficient. Go and seek help and advice from your student union or a student counsellor or your tutor or a member of the law department, if there's one on your college campus. If you'd rather not discuss the matter on campus, try your local citizens advice bureau or local law centre. (Both numbers should be in the *Yellow Pages* phone book). There may be technical points of law on which you're completely ignorant. Take the relevant letters, documents or court orders with you. If you really are in legal trouble, and have to make a court appearance, you're going to need the urgent help and advice of a sympathetic, available, professionally qualified person. Don't delay. You need to act as soon as you become aware of the problem. Finally, if you have to be away from college for any time in connection with some legal matter, tell the college authorities. You don't have to tell them the details if you choose not to.

When you really can't face it ...

Every college teacher at some time in his or her career is confronted by one or more students who say they're proposing to drop out because they simply can't face college life any longer. Maybe that's a wise and mature decision, taken after proper consideration of all the right issues from all the right angles. There's no shame attached to dropping out, if you find you've made a genuine mistake about college. Perhaps college is just not for you – or you're not right for this particular college! Whichever way, you've still your whole life ahead of you. Leaving college is a serious decision, fraught with consequences – but it's not the end of the world.

Try to keep things in proportion. One bad set of exam marks, one botched relationship, one more insolvency – or all three together – should not lead to a hasty decision to pack your bags and leave. If you're feeling depressed and you attribute your feelings to your college life, you'll naturally feel like getting out and moving away. But that may not be the best decision in all circumstances. For example, if you're not functioning properly, there could be some physical or emotional cause which is hidden from view. In any event, you should never contemplate dropping out of college without taking time out to discuss the pros and cons of withdrawal with a member of college staff. In most colleges, there's provision for intermitting (i.e. taking some time out of college with formal written consent for some genuine personal reason) without spoiling your chances of returning when you feel ready to do so. A serious illness or accident may require a medical intermission in your studies. So may a family or personal problem, a bereavement, whether a death or the end of a marriage or similar relationship.

Don't ever drop out of college without talking things over first. You owe it to yourself. You owe it to your family. You owe it to those who care about you at college. Give your college the benefit of the doubt and go and see a counsellor or member of staff today. Don't make the decision during a vacation and, above all, don't try to make the decision alone. It could well be the wrong decision – in which case you might regret it for the rest of your life.

In short, whatever your problem – however serious or however trivial – if it's worrying you in a way which prevents you from eating, sleeping or working, go and see somebody qualified to offer you confidential help. That person is often a stone's throw away. Don't go without seeing them first. If only to say goodbye!

SUGGESTIONS FOR FURTHER READING

National Union of Students, *Welfare Manual*, London: NUS, annually (phone 01–272–8900)

University of Strathclyde Students' Association *Welfare Manual*, Glasgow, USSA, annually (phone 041–552–1895)

Consult your College or University Student Services Dept. Counselling Service, Student Advisory Service, Health Centre, Chaplaincy etc.

22 Career choice and job search*

> *The correspondence between a man's place in the
> university class-list and his ultimate place in the later
> course of his life may be an induced and artificial
> correspondence: in other words, the fact of what is
> called a 'good honours degree' may be the cause of
> obtaining a good and lucrative post ... For myself I
> should never grade men in their thirties or forties or
> fifties by what they did in their early twenties. I should
> grade them afresh, on every occasion when grading
> was necessary, on the evidence before me at the time.
> A university degree is not a label for life.*
>
> Ernest Barker, *Age and Youth* (1953)

*This chapter was kindly contributed by Ian Easton, MA, FIPM, Career Counsellor and Senior Partner, Career Choice and Job Search, to whom any comments and queries on this chapter may be directly addressed at the University of Strathclyde Business School, Rotten Row, Glasgow G4 OLN, Scotland, marking your envelope 'Confidential'.

This chapter tries to do three things:

1. To explain the importance of a strategic approach to career choice and job search.
2. To suggest ways of thinking about getting a job and building a satisfying career.
3. To offer some hints about job applications and job interviews.

THE IMPORTANCE OF A STRATEGIC APPROACH

Most students, both home and overseas, undergraduates and post-graduates, invest much time, money and effort on securing their academic qualifications – but few devote many resources to purposeful thinking about their likely future careers. Even good students with an impressive school and college track-record, tend to assume that an academic qualification confers an automatic passport to a good job and a successful career of their choice. They quickly become disabused when they begin their job search.

Students who fail to adopt a strategic approach to their careers frequently become disillusioned in their new jobs, fail to develop satisfying careers and engage in 'job-swapping'. This wasteful effort reflects poorly not only on the students themselves but also on their qualifying institutions. Mounting evidence from colleges in Britain and the USA conclusively supports the view that all students need professional guidance on how to adopt a strategic approach to their career planning.

A strategic approach conserves energy by focusing on what you really want and need from your future career; by closely examining your achievements and disappointments; by clarifying the fundamental values that steer your life; and by ensuring you concentrate your efforts in areas where you are more likely to enjoy your work and therefore do well at it.

As well as seeking help in preparing a professional CV (or résumé), in searching for job vacancies, in writing effective job applications and practising interview skills, most students greatly benefit from confidential and sensitive counselling sessions at which they have the opportunity to conduct a careful, detailed evaluation of their careers to date, to explore personal aims and career aspirations, and to assess the chances of their achieving satisfaction and success in their chosen areas of career specialization.

GETTING A JOB AND BUILDING A CAREER

A job of work is not a career. There are lots of job vacancies to be filled but only some hold out the prospect of a satisfying long-term career for the job-holders. They are a means to an end: getting the bank manager off your back, keeping the wolf from the door. A career contains three added dimensions:

1.   Greater continuity through time.
2.   The promise of personal growth.
3.   Intrinsic psychological satisfaction as well as extrinsic economic rewards and material success.

What makes a career satisfying and rewarding ultimately depends on individual tastes, interests, aptitudes and – above all – self-knowledge. In other words, you need to spend time getting to know your deep-felt needs and wants first, before you go racing out into the job market, competing for jobs of the kind you may not even want and are not qualified to do.

So, what do you need to know about yourself?

1.   What kind of things do you really enjoy doing? The chances are that the things we enjoy most are those at which we do best. This is not an invariable rule, but it's a good start. You'll probably be in your chosen career for many years – so you might as well enjoy what you choose to do.
2.   What independent evidence is there that you really do these things well? Consider the kind of tasks you've been congratulated by others for doing well, or the tasks for which you've received commendation or special praise.
3.   List some of the more significant achievements and disappointments in your life to date – and consider carefully how these experiences have shaped your attitudes to work and rewards.
4.   Think carefully about those fundamental values that you cherish most in life – whatever their source: religion, upbringing, political beliefs, etc. These are unlikely to change much in adult life – so you need to clarify your values for your own sake, before you attempt to build your career.
5.   Examine the range of possible careers open to men and women these days. Give yourself time and opportunity to explore some of the newer or less-familiar career possibilities. Reject nothing at this stage – you need to give yourself the widest possible chance.

6. Go out to talk to men and women who are established in the careers that interest you. Try to discover what it is they find both rewarding and frustrating about their work. Ask yourself whether you have the necessary skills, knowledge and temperament that would allow you to enjoy that career. Don't ask them directly for a job – but tell them what you're looking for – and don't be afraid to ask their advice.

HINTS ABOUT JOB APPLICATIONS AND JOB INTERVIEWS

Your job application is your 'visiting card' – so it has to be immaculate. If you simply scrawl a note, asking for an application form, that piece of evidence about you could well finish up on your personal file and reduce your chances of securing a job. Never use fancy notepaper or coloured ink – unless, perhaps, you're a graphic artist/designer seeking to place your talents on immediate display. Take a copy of everything you send and start a new file for each potential employer.

Your application should be concise and relevant. It should clearly indicate the vacancy for which you are applying and then refer to an enclosed curriculum vitae (CV) or résumé. The CV or résumé should ideally be tailor-made for the particular job vacancy. A pre-printed CV is normally acceptable for more junior jobs but with more senior jobs, you should aim to prepare a CV or résumé for that specific job.

A CV is the most important document you'll prepare in your entire career, therefore it's worth taking the utmost pains to get it just right. It needs to be drafted, edited, re-read in the light of a new day, again edited and then proof-read and corrected until it approaches perfection.

Classic format for British-style CV
(As opposed to more job-targeted American-style résumé):

CURRICULUM VITAE OF _____ _____
(Name in BLOCK CAPITALS)

1. Full name (in block capitals):
    (including maiden name, if married/divorced/widowed)
2. Date of birth:
    (British: day/month/year; American: month/day/year)
3. Place of birth:
    (city/state)
4. Nationality:
    (whether by birth or other qualification)

5. Marital status:
   (e.g. single/married/separated/divorced/widowed)
6. Family:
   (names of children and dates of birth, not current ages)
7. Education:
   (in chronological order, showing schools, colleges attended and standards achieved)
8. Employment record:
   (including vacation work, if any, in chronological order)
9. Special attainments (if any):
   (including fluency in foreign languages, prizes, special distinctions, etc.)
10. Leisure interests:
    (not necessarily a complete list)

Application forms

If you're invited to complete the organization's prescribed application form, be equally meticulous over details. There's almost invariably a question asking you to present a pen-portrait of yourself, or to outline and evaluate your career to date, or to give some indication of your career aspirations. Make several drafts and edit ruthlessly before committing yourself in writing. Make sure you take a copy – and be ready to answer supplementary questions at interview.

Attending the job interview

A job interview is a conversation with a purpose, namely, to allow both you and a potential employer to decide whether you are the best applicant for the job vacancy. You should treat the job interview like any other business meeting. Take your file and have it to hand throughout the interview, for ease of reference. You should not be afraid to consult your file, just as the interviewer(s) will do.

There are six key points you need to remember about successful job interviews:

1. First impressions *do* count. Most interviewers tend to make up their minds about candidates within the first few minutes and don't normally change their minds. It pays to be dressed and groomed in context. Tailored suits are in; nose jewels out.
2. You need to tell the interviewer what you can do for the organization, not what you expect the organization to do for you.
3. You need to 'sell' yourself during the first half of the interview and not lose the job in the second half. Imply more than you say.
4. You need to get across three or four key selling points about yourself, directly relevant to the job, which persuade the

interviewers in your favour. For example, the job concerns the Channel Tunnel? Your mother is French. You are bilingual. The job involves travel to the Far East? You grew up in a British diplomatic family in Hong Kong. The work involves nuclear energy risks? You are a lifelong supporter of safe nuclear energy policies. The job is located in Scunthorpe? Your uncle is the local MP. The organization expects you to be mobile? You have no current plans to start a family.

5. Most interviews follow a fairly predictable pattern:

   (a) *Early pleasantries* – to put you at ease and set the tone.
   (b) *Biographical review* – often an invitation to take the interviewer through the more significant points of your career to date. Be ready for this.
   (c) *Direct questions* – asking you, for example:

       (i)   Why do you want the job?
       (ii)   Why do you think you're qualified to do the job?
       (iii) Why do you think you'd be good at the job?
       (iv)   What do you already know about the job or the organization?
       (v)   How would you like to see the job develop over the next three to five years?

   (d) *Indirect questions* – asking you, for example:

       (i)   Whether you're free to take up the job, if offered?
       (ii)   Whether you have any questions to ask about the job?
       (iii) What job do you see yourself doing in the next five years?

   (e) *Concluding remarks* – such as:

       (i)   thanking you for coming;
       (ii)   saying when you may expect to hear the outcome;
       (iii) inviting you to claim your travel expenses.

6 The employer is hiring you for your personality, your enthusiasm, your trained mind, your capacity to learn, to adapt and to help him or her solve tomorrow's problems – not just today's.

Finally, give no hostages to fortune, make everything you write and say about yourself sound as positive as possible. In these days of high graduate unemployment in Mrs Thatcher's Britain, it's worth remembering the words of Sir James Barrie: 'You've forgotten the greatest moral attribute of a Scotsman, Maggie, that he'll do nothing which might damage his career.' (*What Every Woman Knows*, Act II). Good luck and successful job hunting!

SUGGESTIONS FOR FURTHER READING

Bolles, R.N., *What Colour is your Parachute?* California: Ten Speed Press, UK ed, annually
CRAC, *Graduate Employment and Training*, Cambridge: Hobsons Publishing, annually
GO, *Graduate Opportunties*, London: Newpoint Publishing, annually

23 Staying on at college*

Linbov Andreevna: Are you still a student?
Trofimov: I expect I shall be a student to the end of my days.

Anton Chekhov, *The Cherry Orchard* (1904)

This chapter tries to do three things:

1. To explore the reasons why students stay on at college.
2. To help you decide whether you should stay on.
3. To examine how you should go about staying on.

WHY STUDENTS STAY ON

The vast majority of students are happy to graduate at the end of their chosen course of study – and will never visit their college again, except perhaps for a reunion or a sentimental journey. But each year a

*Grateful thanks are expressed to Professor John Midgley and Dr Carolyn Converse, Department of Pharmacy, University of Strathclyde, for help and collaboration in the writing of this chapter.

growing minority of well-qualified students decide that, in a world in which many more of their contemporaries hold a first degree, it's no bad thing to take their studies further by qualifying for some postgraduate diploma, vocational qualification or higher degree.

For example, with a good bachelor of arts, science or engineering degree, you may feel ready to compete for jobs and start your career in civil engineering, banking, insurance, commerce, the off-shore oil industry, the civil service or whatever takes your fancy. But for some graduates, especially those who have done well on an honours course (typically, with a first or an upper second), there will be a strong temptation to stay on to do research.

What does research or study for a higher degree entail?
Many students are attracted to the idea of taking a higher degree. Others find research very satisfying and welcome the opportunity to spend several years engrossed in this fascinating activity. Some will aim for the highest level of postgraduate research, namely, the PhD (or DPhil or doctor of philosophy) degree. Others will be satisfied with a masters degree (a 'taught masters' or a 'research masters'). What do these choices entail?

The 'taught masters', as its name implies, follows very similar lines to an honours degree, with lectures, tutorials and seminars, culminating in a research dissertation/project report at the end of one or two years. The 'research masters' differs from the 'taught masters' in one significant respect: most of the work comprises your own research. There may be academic seminars or classes in research methodology, project planning or dissertation writing but you will be working very largely on your own, under the overall guidance of an academic supervisor.

The normal PhD/DPhil programme lasts for three years. Ideally, the first two or two and a half years are spent becoming acquainted with the literature in your field of specialization and working on a research project in a laboratory (if you're an applied scientist), or working up your draft outline (if you're an arts or social science student). A thesis is then written on the completed research and, after an oral examination, the degree may be awarded.

What are the entry qualifications for a higher degree?
Normally, postgraduate studentships are limited to upper seconds and first-class honours students. Although there are problems in finding financial support for candidates with a 2 (ii) degree, some holders of 2 (ii) degrees have been admitted to the PhD/DPhil course (MSc or MPhil research) and have proved to be very successful research students.

In the past, academic departments were allotted a number of studentships by various government-sponsored research councils.

There were 'quota' awards for departments with strong research reputations and 'pool' awards for students with good first degrees. During recent years, however, many research councils have had their research budgets severely cut by government and have been forced, in turn, to restrict to a minimum the number of quota and pool awards they dispense.

Departments fortunate enough to receive quota awards may subsequently apply, if necessary, for additional funds from various scientific, literary or philosophical societies. In addition, individual members of academic staff may have research grants that include support for postgraduate students. In faculties of science, business or technology, departments are normally able to find some form of financial support for well-qualified PhD students. In faculties of arts and social science, art, music and drama, departments may have the very greatest difficulty in helping even the best-qualified students to find financial support.

Some research grants include money to pay the salary of a postgraduate research assistant. These are university employees, yet they may register for a PhD (or another higher degree) and will not normally be charged any fees, as long as they stay on the university payroll. It's worth while finding out whether any such positions are open, as the financial benefits may be substantial.

How do you know if you're suited for research?
Aside from a natural curiosity and desire to find out, in greater depth, what 'makes things tick', it's hard to describe the attributes of a good research worker. Steady plodders are not necessarily superior to excitable, enthusiastic people with their temperamental ups and downs. Those who are 'all thumbs' in undergraduate labs may become good experimentalists, given more time to develop their laboratory technique. Those who experienced difficulty in verbalizing their undergraduate ideas on complex problems within the fields of philosophy, economics, history or literature, may nevertheless write original and ingenious dissertations within their chosen disciplines, given helpful postgraduate supervision.

How do I choose a postgraduate supervisor?
The first step, of course, is to pick a subject within a field that genuinely interests you and that you would like to pursue. Then, it's probably advisable to talk to all the people you can who work in that field, before you make up your mind. Points worth considering are:

1. *The past record of the supervisor* Is his or her work well thought of? Have his or her past students had particular problems with their projects that might have been avoided?

2. *The working environment* Is the necessary equipment available? Are there other people (postgrads, postdocs, senior technicians) to help you when your supervisor is absent or busy? It might be advisable to have a frank discussion with them.
3. *The project itself* Do you think it is well thought of? Will you actually enjoy doing this research? If you have any doubts, it's best to discuss them with your potential supervisor before you start. Sometimes, joint supervision, shared between two members of staff, or a staff member and an outside specialist (e.g. industry, hospital or other institution) may be arranged.

It's important to recognize that the choice of supervisor is sometimes limited by availability of funds, and that heads of departments (or divisions in large departments) must exercise some discretion in the distribution of research students amongst members of staff, particularly when quota awards or other central funds are involved.

Most departments will have prepared a listing of the research interests of their staff members, normally obtainable from the departmental office. After consultation with the head of department or adviser of postgraduate students, you may decide to transfer to another college for PhD or other training – simply because the best person to supervise your research works there. In any event, it's essential to go to discuss your proposed research with that person – and to consider the uses to which you might wish to put the research when it is successfully completed (see also Chapter 14 on writing a research dissertation or project report).

What's the use of a postgraduate qualification?
The following case studies may offer the best answer to that question.

Postgraduate case study 23. 1 Suzanne was a mature student who last year successfully completed an ordinary BA from a provincial university, alongside hundreds of other students who had decided not to do honours. Married, aged 30, with two school-age sons, Suzanne did not rate very highly her chances of landing a good job unless she could offer her potential employer something more than the intellectual training of her first degree. With her husband's agreement and support, she registered for a postgraduate diploma in Information Science, a one-year course that would open up for her the new and exciting world of information technology. Not everyone's choice, certainly, but one that Suzanne found attractive and rewarding.

The first point to be made about postgraduate studies is that your motivation must be positive. Staying on to undertake further studies simply because you've nothing better to do is anathema. Who knows, you might discover an interest in some subject! But you might become terribly disillusioned and wish you'd taken your chances on the job market after your first degree.

Postgraduate case study 23. 2 Michael surprised his friends at the University of York by pulling off a 2 (i) degree in Economics, with a special interest in financial management. His tutor encouraged him to stay on to read for a one-year full-time taught masters degree in Economics, with the prospect of writing a dissertation on the acquisition policies of overseas multinationals, with special reference to the British confectionery industry. (Michael had spent two of his summer vacations working part time for Rowntree's of York, where his father had spent his entire working life on the shopfloor.) This combination of academic and personal motivation helped Michael sustain his enthusiasm for his subject and eventually led him to Brussels where he now works for the European High Commission as a Senior Economist in Marketing Studies.

The second point to be made about postgraduate studies is that you should try to talk the matter through very carefully with the most sympathetic teacher in the department where you wish to continue your studies. Most departments allocate responsibility for postgraduate students to an adviser of postgraduate studies. He or she will normally offer a frank opinion on whether you seem capable of sustaining the physical and intellectual energy needed to complete another year (two years, in some cases) at college on postgraduate work. Don't be surprised or offended if you're advised to spend some time in a working environment first – and then return for a postgraduate course of study at some later date.

Postgraduate case study 23. 3 Rowena was a widow, with three children all at primary school, when she was transferred from the Open University into the third year of a more traditional degree in science. Having successfully completed her finals, she felt unable to devote herself to full-time employment because of her domestic responsibilities. After careful thought and advice, she registered for a one-year full-time postgraduate diploma in Career Guidance and Employent Counselling – a field of great interest to her and one in which she could work full time during normal school hours, keeping normal school terms. Rowena was shortly on her way to helping school-leavers solve their own career problems.

The third point to be made about postgraduate studies is that you should certainly have a much better idea where such studies might lead you in career terms than you had when embarking on your first degree. A potential employer will question why you chose a particular field of postgraduate study, to check your motivation and commitment, before hiring you into a responsible job in that field. The more vocational the more postgraduate course of studies, the more sure you need to be that you're in the right field. Seek professional careers guidance – and explore financial grants – before taking a firm decision.

Postgraduate case study 23. 4. Philip left college immediately after taking a 'good honours degree' in History at Sussex. He made his way to a college of higher education where he carried out research into school curriculum development in mainland Scotland. This led him to complete an MA degree, followed by five years teaching History in a local comprehensive school. In his seventh year after college, he took stock of his career and decided to requalify for a career in the private sector of business. Taking voluntary redundancy from teaching, he began a one-year full-time MBA course at Strathclyde Business School where he sought counselling from Career Choice and Job Search, a confidential continuing employment counselling service. On the strength of advice received, assistance with preparing a modern-style résumé, and practice at advanced interview skills, Philip applied for, and was interviewed for, several jobs with large multinationals. He is now a Senior Sales Consultant with Rank Xerox, with responsibilities covering sales throughout Scotland and Northern Ireland.

Every college has different regulations controlling admission to higher degree courses and courses of study leading to vocational qualifications or (possible partial exemption from) professional examinations. Demand for places is high and the competition is strong. You should, therefore, register your interest at several well-researched and well-resourced colleges as soon as possible *in the preceding academic year*. Do not assume you will automatically be offered a place at the postgraduate institution of your first choice. Be realistic and be ready to compromise. London is an increasingly more expensive, crowded and dirty city in which to live and study than many others in Britain. And you should certainly consider well-respected institutions overseas – such as the European business schools or those in selected parts of the USA.

SUGGESTIONS FOR FURTHER READING

CRAC, *The Students' Guide to Graduate Studies in the UK*, Cambridge, Hobsons Publishing, annually

DOG, *Directory of Opportunities for Graduates*, London: Newpoint Publishing, annually

24 So, what did you get out of college?

*Life is a voyage, perilous indeed. But men were not
made for safe harbours*

Edith Hamilton 1867–1963

You're coming to the end of your college days. It may seem only
yesterday that you set out on this voyage of self-discovery. Now you're
about to launch yourself into the wider world, with greater risks and
opportunities ahead. It's worth taking time to consider just what you
got out of your college experience.

A LIFELONG LOVE OF LEARNING?

Whatever their personal feelings on entering college, by the time they
graduate most students discover that their lives have undergone a
profound transformation – which inevitably colours the rest of their
private and their working lives. Though their shadows may never
again darken college doors – though they may feel profoundly
overjoyed to be putting college behind them and getting out into the
world – most graduates still look back on their college days with pride
and affection. Never again will they pick up a newspaper or a book,

see a film or play, or take part in intelligent conversation without some more or less conscious indebtedness to their college experience. That's because college is not simply concerned with gaining knowledge or acquiring skill. Much more importantly, it's concerned with how we view our world and the ways in which we want to see it changed. Once the 'learning bug' is in our bloodstream, we can never stop learning or wanting to learn. In effect, the college experience has imperceptibly transformed our lives – and in irreversible ways. We can never be the same again.

A PASSPORT TO A JOB?

If you're canny as well as intelligent, you'll have given time and careful thought to the type of work you're likely to do best at after college. Better still, you'll have taken professional guidance or sought counselling on this critical matter. Official statistics confirm our common observation that many of the most-rewarding and best-paid jobs in advanced technological societies – as well as those in developing countries – go to those with higher education qualifications. Provided you've chosen your subjects and options with care and an eye to the future, your college training should prove invaluable in helping you secure the favourable attention of employers.

What employers hire, after all, is not merely their employees' academic qualifications but their experience, their character, their potentiality – for fast learning, for contributing ideas, for generating imaginative and workable solutions to practical problems, for self-motivation, self-discipline and a professional pride in achievement – a job well done. Writing a sales or market report or making a presentation on your analysis of a complex organizational problem, with recommendations for action – these paid employment tasks are not so very different from writing final-year essays or preparing a dissertation or project report. So, your college experience and academic qualifications may well prove a passport to a good job and a consistently rewarding career.

AN INTELLECTUAL TRAINING?

For some proportion of each year's college graduates, the excitement of intellectual enquiry will lead them to stay on at college to pursue further studies in preparation for a higher degree or some form of professional or vocational training. Even those who leave will have gained an intellectual training they carry with them through the rest of their lives. When faced with a personal or career problem, college graduates make use of that intellectual training which has become an unconscious part of their being. They can no more help being 'intellectual' than they can help breathing. This carries with it certain attendant risks – such as losing touch with those members of our family or friends who may not have had the same opportunity or desire to go to college. There is also the risk of intellectual arrogance and intolerance towards those who may not have had the privilege of going through higher education. College graduates would do well to remember that knowledge is not to be equated with wisdom and that education does not automatically confer character.

A SET OF SOCIAL SKILLS?

As noted earlier, college offers a shared learning experience. During the course of your college work, you've shared lectures, tutorials and seminars and experienced the common bond of academic life – the struggle to find relevant books and articles, to shape your ideas into a coherent structure for an essay or class presentation. Then there have been all those non-work occasions when you've interacted successfully (or otherwise) with fellow students and college staff: coffee breaks, refectory lunches, tea and sympathy, late-night parties – with strong coffee the following morning.

Without being conscious of the process, you've acquired and polished a serviceable set of social skills that should enable you to relate easily to most other people throughout the rest of your life. For, whether you join a multinational corporation, a local health authority, a medium-sized firm or set up your own small business, the secret of success in contemporary working life is co-operation – with clients, suppliers, customers and fellow employees at all levels. These social and communication skills are amongst the valuable assets you'll take away from college life – and they weren't on a single prospectus or class syllabus!

A SENTIMENTAL EDUCATION?

If you're wise – and normally healthy and lucky – you'll have taken advantage of being at college to explore relationships with members of the opposite (or same) sex and formed close friendships, whether they survive college or not. Again, without necessarily realizing it, you'll have undergone an education of the heart as well as the head. Flaubert called it 'a sentimental education' – the graduated experience of coping with love – the most exquisite and painful of all adult emotions.

You'll have made mistakes – perhaps too many to mention. Never mind. If you can't trust yourself to learn from your mistakes at college, when can you? Once more, that learning experience will stand you in good stead as you go out into the world of wider opportunities and an even wider range of human relationships and emotions. There's a time for regret and a time for tears. But there's also a time for courage and optimism. Let's hope your sentimental education has equipped you, to some degree, to cope with affairs of the heart as you make your way to the heart of affairs.

SOME GOOD FRIENDS?

College friendships endure remarkably. The present writer cherishes several such friendships that have survived and matured down the forty or so years since he first left college. As an inveterate optimist, you'll naturally try to keep in touch with those close friends you've made at college. You may plan to attend annual reunions your college may organize. But don't underestimate the extent to which natural life-forces – work, marriage, family, health – may lead even close college friends to drift apart. It's easy to lose touch, so make up your mind to sustain the effort to keep in touch with significant others.

These guidenotes were written to help you survive and succeed at college. We hope you've found them useful throughout your college experience. If you have, we'd be very glad to hear from you.

If you have any ideas or constructive suggestions for improving this text in any way for the benefit of those who follow in your footsteps, please drop us a line. We'll be delighted to hear from you. Please complete the tear-out form on page 167 and mail it to the address given. Thank you.

Now, as you leave college and go out into the world, we wish you all the luck in the world!

Index

To   Sander Meredeen
      c/o Paul Chapman Publishing Limited
      144 Liverpool Road
      Islington
      London N1 1LA

From:
Address:
Subject: *Study for Survival and Success*
Date:

I have read your book and should like to offer the following comments

What I like most about the book is:

What I like least about the book is:

What I'd like to see in the book is: